ARNOLD BENNETT IN LOVE

Comarques from an aquatint by Arnold Bennett

Arnold Bennett in Love

*Arnold Bennett
and his wife
Marguerite Soulié
A Correspondence*

Edited and translated by
GEORGE & JEAN BEARDMORE

823.912 BEN

DAVID BRUCE & WATSON
LONDON

© GEORGE AND JEAN BEARDMORE 1972

First published in 1972 by
DAVID BRUCE AND WATSON LIMITED
44 Great Russell Street
London   WC1

SBN 85127 - 008 - 5

Printed in Great Britain at
The Compton Press
Salisbury

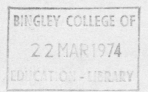

CONTENTS

PLATES

A Late Victorian

Although this story has a beginning in a proposal of marriage, and a development that includes wealth, celebrity, and such accessories as a yacht and a country house, and a climax that comes of collision between two strong personalities, it is neither a biography nor a novel but a documentary, the distillation of over a quarter of a million words into a comprehensive narrative, in which the two principal characters tell their own story by means of letters.

However, even documentaries must have backgrounds, and this one has its roots in Victorian England, in the middle of the 1850s, when a precocious boy of twelve was put out to work in a pottery. The entire district was known as the Potteries, a hilly region in North Staffordshire otherwise given up to coal-mines and ironworks, and a hundred years ago as isolated and self-sufficient as a valley in Iran. Over the centuries it had created its own dialect, stamped out its own species—some ten inches shorter than elsewhere, dark, broad-shouldered with the wielding of picks, pockmarked with coal or white with clay-dust, often deformed or with fingers missing, often debilitated with silicosis or lead-poisoning or watery-eyed with watching kiln-fires—and sorted out its own sharply defined strata of society. In the absence of reasonable housing and effective Trade Unions, society had sought to protect itself from the effects of beer and disease with a fervid Methodism, which by its constitutions could never be allowed to lapse into the ritual of more orthodox churches.

This boy of twelve, Enoch Bennett, was the son of a dedicated Wesleyan who was also a Sunday School Superintendent, who had knowingly, because he himself was a potter, thrust the child out into conditions we should now call inhuman and among men and women whom we should regard as brutalised. They were not the lowest of the low because they possessed hereditary skills and beneath them were immigrant Welsh and Irish labourers, but above them were ranged a lower middle-class of small shop-keepers, clerks, and teachers, a middle class of businessmen, doctors, solicitors, bankers, and architects, and over all an aristocracy of employers.

Few escaped their caste, and the father, John, was incredulous when this potter's boy, Enoch, said that he wanted to be a solicitor. He refused him not because the idea was absurd but because law was of the Devil. However, Enoch was already showing exceptional mental powers, and John apprenticed him to a schoolmaster at £5 a year.

Eventually Enoch became a schoolmaster himself but he never abandoned the ambition to become a solicitor, and when he came of age and his father died he began systematically to read law. He read law solidly for twelve years and meanwhile to make money he left teaching to become a partner in a small pottery firm. He married. The pottery failed and he raised the capital to become a pawnbroker. Babies began to appear and he was compelled to move from slum-dwelling to slum-dwelling, such as the two-up and two-down of John Street, Burslem, which at the back had a privy across the yard and at the front opened directly on to the pavement of a small alley. Enoch heroically went on reading law until he passed his first examination and went to serve his time as an articled clerk, after which more reading was necessary until at age thirty-four, in 1876, he was admitted as a solicitor.

None of this detail of social history and murderous endeavour would have the slightest interest but that Enoch's first-born was Arnold Bennett, one of the three popular 'greats' in the literature of the first quarter of this century.[1] Arnold was a regional novelist who created the Five Towns out of his native Potteries; a playwright; a journalist of great influence; and a man of immense mental and moral power.

Arnold's marriage and his attitude towards the extrovert Frenchwoman who became his wife are only understandable if one bears in mind that as an infant he had experienced the smelly little rooms and brick closet; he had witnessed the pregnancies and the three still-births; he had seen the strings of drying nappies and underwear overhead as he had lain in his cot; he had been aware from his first conscious moment of the irascible presence in the locked room. True, the family eventually moved into a villa in Waterloo Road outside the town but by then Arnold was eleven years old and the trauma had been inflicted.

---

[1] Whether they are today regarded as the three 'greats' is open to question: Henry James, Joseph Conrad, D. H. Lawrence, and George Moore were their contemporaries.

One wonders if Marguérite ever realised that in marrying Arnold she had married an extension into the twentieth century of a Victorian husband—that Arnold was in fact an extension of Enoch. Both men were ruled exclusively by the head, both were utterly sure of themselves and sacrificed all and everything for their work, both were contemptuous of failure, unpunctuality, and ignorance, both were bred in the northern tradition that wives did as they were told and existed only to serve their masters.

Arnold's mother, for example, used to listen out half-an-hour before Enoch was expected home from work, and when the tap with the signet-ring came at the front door, she would run to open it, she would help him off with his coat, she would kneel at his feet to unlace his boots and replace them with the slippers she had carefully put to warm an hour before. Figuratively speaking, Arnold was expecting the same service from Marguérite forty years later—and she was a Frenchwoman from the south ! Because he was a thinking man and prided himself on his liberal views, he told himself : 'I will make my wife as generous an allowance as I can, and give her all the freedom she wants,' but his instinct was to keep her at home and have her kneel to put on his slippers.

He allowed her a flat of her own, freedom to travel and entertain as she liked, and munificent pin-money, but on the other hand she was to write (7th August 1918): 'To please you, I will cease to argue and discuss, and I will try to fit in with your principle, that I ought only to listen and obey,' which in varying words had been the burden of most of her complaints, and which in the last analysis was to break the marriage.

The most painful characteristic of every member of the Bennett family, except the children's mother, was the absence of any sort of sentiment. Tenderness had been rooted out, crushed, and burnt in the interest of intellect. None of them knew what love was or, if they did, they were at pains to hide it, and they went on to instruct their children how to hide it, too, sometimes successfully. Kisses, the raptures of youth, the poetry and the ingenuousness of early boyhood and girlhood—these were so unknown that when observed in others they excited as much derision as if they had rubbed noses. Those six Bennett children were never allowed to be young. "Sustained effort" and "duty" were the first words impressed upon them. A dictionary stood on the breakfast-table.

11

After high tea on Saturdays Enoch assembled all six children in the dining-room with the object of holding a general knowledge test. 'The competitions,' Arnold wrote, 'included the whole field of knowledge . . . Instead of a stopwatch he relied on his ear and on his autocratic authority.'[2] At whatever age, the children were forbidden outside the house after dark.

The intense experience of being dominated, ridiculed, and thrashed by Enoch is still making itself felt two if not three generations later: among his grandchildren handsome girls have remained unmarried, brothers and sisters are estranged, and cousins would not recognize one another if they met in the street. Unfortunately for the Bennetts, love will out, and when a deliberate campaign is waged against it, it notoriously turns on the persecutors. Arnold, for example, suffered all his life from neuralgia, insomnia, and stomach upsets, real or psychosomatic, while his most public affliction was a stammer which, in moments of crisis (as we shall see), contorted his face into a terrifying snarl. But at least this stammer had the effect of making him prefer to write to his wife, rather than speak to her directly, which is the reason for the existence of many of the succeeding letters.

What of his brothers and sisters? To one, George Beardmore, the youngest of the four children born to Arnold's eldest sister, Sissie, those Bennett aunts and uncles were terrifying phenomena. One hid from them. At least, I did, as a child. I even tried to hide from my own mother, rarely with success. After her death in 1939 (eight years after Arnold, that is) we children listed sixteen public offices she had held, starting as a certificated midwife and going on to become a Red Cross quartermaster, president of the local British Womens' Temperance Association (how those initials 'B.W.T.A.' became printed on my infant mind!), District Food Officer during World War One, chairman of this and that committee (oh, those gatherings of rustling skirts in the front room!) and capping all by being made one of the nation's first women magistrates.

Oddly enough, nobody remembers her now. When I revisit the

[2] From an unpublished article 'My Education' at Keele University.

Potteries sundry elderly natives may ask me : 'You are Frank's son, aren't you?' or 'What happened to your father, after all?' but rarely, if ever, concern themselves with my mother. Yet he had flung his patrimony, like Palissy, into the furnaces of his small pot-bank in Fenton (the forgotten Sixth Town), been declared bankrupt, and had the furniture of his home bought for £500 with typical generosity by Arnold Bennett, who then handed it back into Sissie's care. It is this failed, undefeated man, who refused at a much later date to enter Arnold's flat in Chiltern Court out of some unknowable other-generation dislike—it is this man who is remembered.

Frank, the older of Arnold's two brothers, became a solicitor like their father and moved to Rochdale. I have no recollection of meeting him until, mystified by the repeated warning that under no circumstances must I lend him money, I found him flying a kite on Bognor beach. He didn't ask for money and I took rather a liking to him, a small figure with a very red skin showing through white hair and beard who crackled with witticisms ('If you aren't careful,' he said, artfully handling two kites on one string, 'I shall let you fly these kites'). He died of double pneumonia as a result of alcoholic poisoning. It was this brother's eldest son Richard, whom, as we shall see, Marguérite took under her wing.[8]

In Arnold's revealing letter to Marguérite of 15th February 1907, he confides his fears that he will soon have to pay for the divorce of a sister from her husband. This was Emily (or Emilie) Vernon. His third sister, Tertia, is often mentioned. (She, I think, must be the sister also mentioned in this letter to whom he is paying 'a certain sum'.) Following a bathing tragedy at Criccieth, in Wales, in which her fiancé was drowned, Tertia married William Kennerley, a barrister in the Civil Service. Arnold often visited the Kennerleys' home in Clarendon Road, Putney. Tertia was perhaps his closest confidante and certainly his severest critic, and it was to William that Arnold dedicated *The Old Wives' Tale*.

No mention occurs in the letters of the youngest brother, Septimus, a modeller and designer who was possibly the most brilliant, and certainly the most engaging, of the six children. Long

[8] See *Arnold Bennett's Letters to his Nephew*, Richard Bennett (Heinemann 1936).

after he had died, of tuberculosis, my father said sadly : 'I cannot believe that Seppy is dead'.

'I hated,' Arnold wrote a long time later, 'the thought of my youth,' and it is no accident that this most prolific of writers, whose *Journals* are filled with close analyses of behaviour, could never bring himself to write an autobiography. For exactly the same reason I find myself at this moment unable to write about this clever pitiless generation except with difficulty. To be born or to marry into a family of genius is no great cause for envy or celebration.

Outside the home the strongest influence on the children was not that of their school but of the chapel. 'As a child,' the *Times* obituary said, 'he had suffered from the rigours of a strictly religious upbringing which he several times harshly derided'.— Twice every Sunday the Bennett children had been taken to the Hilltop Wesleyan Chapel that their grandfather had helped to found, and at least once again they had been packed off with Arnold in charge to attend Sunday School or a Children's Service. Wesleyanism was not only protecting society, is was also imprinting on their infant minds an indelible sense of guilt against which they were each in their different ways to rebel. Arnold, for example, was to write : 'I see that, at bottom, I have an intellectual scorn, or the scorn of an intellectual man, for all sexual-physical manifestations. I can feel myself despising them at the very moment of deriving satisfaction from them, as if I were playing at being a child.'

Having discovered in himself the absence of love (a word, it will be noted, that he cannot bring himself to use), he had carefully and with the greatest courage set out to teach himself charity, not as one might imagine from the New Testament but from Epictetus and Marcus Aurelius, with the result that he gathered round himself friends and disciples by the dozen.

In a long passage in *Things That Have Interested Me*[4] he wrote :

There is one major satisfaction—and it may well be the greatest of all—which is equally open to all. I mean the exercise of

[4] Chatto and Windus, 1923.

14

benevolence . . . Let both those who can and those who can't do good works make a practice of benevolent *thought*. Let all think kindly of others; never criticize them, never condemn, never judge; on the contrary, let all condone, excuse, justify, seek to comprehend, seek to put themselves in the place of others.

In the course of the letters the reader may look back upon that passage a trifle wryly but the fact remains that, however cold his heart, Arnold was the kindest of men. This is the huge paradox in the man, that he could demonstrably be utterly ruthless when his will was crossed and yet could have his devoted friend, the novelist Frank Swinnerton, say of him : 'His impulse was to help all . . . He had a rich, benevolent, and truly disinterested life of which magnanimity was the keynote.'[5] After his death, Pauline Smith, the South African novelist whom he not so much encouraged as drove to write such neglected masterpieces as *The Little Karoo* and *The Beadle,* described his kindness, patience and altruism in 'A.B. . . . a minor marginal note.'[6] Noel Coward, then the brightest of bright young things, relates how, emanating goodness, Arnold would turn up at rehearsals to cheer up the black moments with a joke. Mrs. Belloc Lowndes, a sister of Hilaire Belloc and authoress of the thriller *The Lodger,* wrote that his most endearing trait was his generous appreciation of other men's work. The list of similar contemporary encomiums is endless. What they testify is true. His nephew, one of the present writers, knows it to be true because it was Arnold who corrected what he called the 'criminal English' of a first novel, *Dodd the Potter,* and recommended it for publication to Cassell & Co. And yet—well, the big 'and yet' will be found in the following letters.

Here, to bring the point home, we are concerned not with friendships but with a marriage, and he had chosen to marry a Frenchwoman from a district not fifty miles from the Spanish frontier who was all spontaneity and impulse, whose instinct, if she thought of going to visit her mother in Toulouse, was to catch the first train there, who liked change, and moving furniture around

[5] From Frank Swinnerton's preface to *Arnold Bennett's Letters to his Nephew.*
[6] Jonathan Cape, 1933.

—one of the most indignant of Arnold's letters came to her on her tenth wedding anniversary when she had moved the piano—and flowers and stylish dresses.

Her French relatives were inclined to say : 'So this is what it's like to be married to an Englishman !' whereas the truth was that she had married a Victorian Englishman of exceptional mental powers who, when any small difficulty arose, was incapable of putting an arm round her and making it up, but instead sat down to reason with her in a four-page letter. As Aldous Huxley put it : 'His relations with women, or rather the women with whom he elected to have relations, require a good deal of explanation.'[7] Such explanation may be found in the following pages.

The Potteries is a difficult place to get away from. Arnold left it when he was twenty-one, and he did not so much leave it as flee from it. He went as a solicitor's clerk and later, when he had proved his competence as a writer, he bought an interest in the periodical *Woman* with money borrowed (according to legend) from his mother. Some time was to pass before, this time borrowing money from his literary agent, James B. Pinker, he went to live and write in France. A case might be made out for the theory that his whole life was spent in flight, that his work was an escape, that even the yacht he bought was a symbol of flight, and that if one asks what he was fleeing from, the answer must be himself. Those twenty years of his slow growth to maturity, so notoriously missing in his biographies, were in fact spent in the painful and assiduous task of burying the Five Towns youth.

As Hamilton Fyfe, a well-known journalist of the day, noted : 'He had not been drawn out : rather had he been pushed in. He had a defective sense of values. He could not in his later years be true to himself, for the reason that he had no solid self to be true to . . . He was amusing, kind, agreeable, but somehow you had a feeling when he had gone or when you had gone, that he had not really been there.'

Another explanation for the defective sense of values may be his preoccupation with writing. No other writer, not even Balzac,

[7] In a letter to James G. Hepburn, an authority on Bennett scholarship. Dr. Hepburn is currently editing Bennett's letters for Oxford University Press.

not even Dickens, so resorted to the pen. It was his narcotic. But nowhere, even in those fascinating Journals, does he lift the veil on himself. One can make only negative deductions, as that children scarcely appear in his books, and that to the natural world, from the lark's nest to the night sky and the wash of the sea, he was blind and deaf. He might personally have been devoid of feeling. Compassion, pity, religious experience, were qualities possessed by others, the outward symptoms of which it was his business to note and accurately portray, like a surveyor who makes a scrupulous inventory of the contents of a room without noting in it the presence of two starving children. His plays, Marguérite remarked in her Journal, failed because they lacked tenderness; she also notes that young people, generous though he was to them, were afraid of him. Marguérite's tragedy was that she could not escape him because love, self-interest, and marriage bound her to him.

At forty-one he was well past the average age when a writer finds himself famous.[8] True, when thirty-three he was making enough money by his short stories, articles, and one novel[9] to be able to throw up the editorship of *Woman* and go to live with his mother, father, and sister Tertia at Hockliffe, in Bedfordshire. But a life in the country was not Arnold and his Journals begin to abound with observations on people met in Paris and London, plays seen, books read, work done, and journeys made, and from 1901 onwards he was living chiefly in Paris. Between then and 1907, when he met Marguérite, he produced at least two novels of note in *Anna of the Five Towns*[10] and *Whom God Hath Joined*[11] but meanwhile he had been mulling over a theme that he intended to turn into a novel greater than any he had written before. At first called *Two Old Women,* this became *The Old Wives' Tale* which was to bring him fame and fortune.

[8] For example, Thomas Hardy with *Under the Greenwood Tree* when thirty-two, D. H. Lawrence with *Sons and Lovers* when twenty-eight. To go farther afield, Balzac was thirty when, after countless pot-boilers, he brought out *Les Derniers Chouans,* and Turgenyev twenty-eight when *A Sportsman's Sketches* appeared. The closest to Arnold in this respect would appear to be John Galsworthy who was thirty-nine when *A Man of Property* brought him recognition.
[9] *A Man from the North* (John Lane, the Bodley Head, 1898).
[10] Chatto and Windus, 1902.
[11] David Nutt, 1906.

The year before he met Marguérite he had suffered a rebuff from a pretty American girl of twenty-five called Eleanor Green to whom he had become engaged with the intention, as he had long ago promised himself, of 'marrying at forty'. Again with money borrowed from Pinker, he had leased and furnished a first-floor flat for the two of them in the rue d'Aumale. Perhaps the prospect of marrying a man by no means young and handsome, and who at that time was neither moneyed nor well-known, had come to intimidate her; perhaps she had caught glimpses of the tyrant within the man of letters, the Enoch within the Arnold, and withdrawn shivering. For whatever reason, she had broken off the engagement.

A few months later, in the spring of 1907, he met Marguérite, and while it can be argued that he married her on the rebound, he was a sensible fellow of forty who, having suffered one disaster, was not likely to court another. But what a difference between the two women! In 1906 did he tell himself : 'Here is a bright attractive girl with money (she was the daughter of an oil-man and sister of the novelist, Julien[12]) whom I can mould to my liking,' and in 1907, having met Marguérite, did he exclaim 'My God, what a woman!'

One can only guess at a man's inmost reflections, even when he is as articulate as Arnold, but it would seem pretty clear that he could only enjoy sexual freedom with women of the theatre. Mention had been made by him in the Journals of a Chichi, a Jeanne, and a Cosette, at least two of whom had been small-time actresses. Although not born to the stage, Marguérite was associated with it.

---

[12] In June, 1971, Julien Green was elected to the *Académie francaise* in succession to Francois Mauriac.

First mention of her occurs in Arnold's Journal under the date, Wednesday, 16th January, 1907:

> When Mdlle Solié called to see me today, she sat after tea on the end of the chaise longue. 'Won't you find an easier seat?' I suggested to her. 'No,' she said, 'I prefer uncomfortable seats. Besides, it gives a feeling of liberty. One is more at one's ease.'

Towards the end of a long life, while tossing crumbs to the ducks and peacocks of her lush run-down estate in the south of France, she was still coming out with remarks like that, and I don't doubt that she captivated Arnold, who in any case was looking for a wife, as she captivated the present writers forty-six years later. She was all of France, and the reverse of everything that was the Potteries, in one person—vital, amusing, handsome rather than pretty (east of Bordeaux, where she was born, a strong Spanish influence is noticeable in dialect, architecture, produce, and in bone-structure) with a great sense of dress and style. She was his phoenix, and even when in later years she was infuriating him, his admiration for her never faltered.

When he first met her she was calling herself 'Solié', possibly to avoid the peasant connotations of 'Soulié'. She was the second child of a baker in Negrepelisse,[1] near Montauban, where the Souliés were at one time in easy circumstances, thanks to a small factory that made and bottled lemonade, soda-water, seltzer-water, and fruit-juices. The baker himself made a separate fortune out of a new kind of stove he invented and patented, and a bread called 'franco-russe', but lost it all and died, a paralysed alcoholic, in an old people's home. Marguérite detested her father, who after losing

[1] Between 1936 and 1950 Marguérite wrote, partly in French and partly in English, a three volume *Résumé de Ma Vie*, a condensation of her Journals, from which much of the ensuing account is taken. Her memory was faulty and she liked in any case to enlarge on truth, for which reason her nephew and executor, M. Etienne Lombrail, has been kind enough to supply a version which more nearly approaches the facts.

his money had deserted his family, but, as we shall see, she took good care of her mother, Juliette.

She was given an exceptional education for a village girl at a convent-school in Toulouse. For this she was indebted to her maternal grandmother, Mme. Hébrard, and Marguérite was to repay her in later years by adopting her name for professional purposes, either as Marguérite Hébrard or as Marguérite Hébrard-Bennett. At an early age she joined an *atelier de couture* called 'Rosalie' in the neighbouring township of St. Antonin. Such ateliers were once common in the towns and villages of provincial France and were useful in absorbing girls of small means like Marguérite. Today they no longer exist.

In view of her subsequent history, let us note here that as a child she had known affluence and later been thrown on to her own resources : if she later became acquisitive and ambitious, this at least is a contributing factor.

Marguérite was already a handsome girl—'*elle s'étiole dans le village*'—and she became bored. A Protestant pastor introduced her as companion to an old infirm lady who commuted between an apartment in Paris and a house near Luchon, in the Hauts Pyrènées. Unfortunately this lady had a predatory husband to escape whom Marguérite left after some months to go back to 'Rosalie'.

But she had visited Paris and tasted enough of the good life to make her want more. 'Rosalie' obtained an opening for her as a model or mannequin to a *grand couturier* in Paris. From model she graduated to *deuxième vendeuse* and later to *première vendeuse*. What fashion-house this was is unknown. Lack of knowledge of English hindered further progress and Marguérite, stamping out the characteristics by which she was to become known, of impulsiveness, daring, and vitality, threw up the job and went to England. First she became *au pair* governess to two small children at the house of a doctor in Felixtowe, Suffolk, and then for a short time a teacher of French at a girls' boarding-school at Richmond, Surrey.

No matter how slight her acquaintance with English still was when she returned to France, the fact that she had stayed in England was later to recommend her to Arnold.

Together with her aunt, Mme Hélène Bion, she now (or at some later date) opened a dress-shop, but the venture failed. With the help of her husband, Georges, Mme Bion went on to make a success of another business: these two must be borne in mind because they were to enter Marguérite's life at a critical moment in her marriage, and unwittingly contribute to its break-up.

Thanks to Mme Bion's intervention, Marguérite found a post with a fashion-house in the rue de la Paix: here, thanks to her English, Marguérite *se stabilise gagnant bien sa vie,* which, roughly translated, means that she began to do all right for herself.

But then she fell in love. He was a law-student of good family who wanted to marry her but, for some reason not stated, was restrained from doing so. The affair lasted three years and his death, we are told, was a sudden enough shock to make her lose her voice and almost her reason. But he left her enough money to give her her freedom, at least for a year or two, and with a view to going on the stage she took lessons in elocution.

Did she in fact succeed in becoming an actress? In the *Résumé* she wrote that her teacher in elocution obtained a part for her as *jeune première* with the impresario, Mayer, for whom she toured the provinces in Alexandre Dumas' play, 'Denise', but in her 'Arnold Bennett' she declared that she abandoned hope of a stage career in favour of marriage.

At the school of elocution she met Blanche Albane, who was later to marry the novelist Georges Duhamel, and through her met Henri Davray, the translator of H. G. Wells and a lifelong friend of Arnold's, Calvocoressi, a music critic and lecturer, and other habitués of the *matinées littéraires* of the day. She affirms that 'Calvo' introduced her to Arnold as his secretary, whereas the truth undoubtedly was that she became his mistress. She was thirty-three and he nearly seven years older, well aware of her past history and present circumstances as his letters and the entries in his Journal testify.

Arnold's Journal, Saturday, 19th January, 1907

Mdlle Solié told me on Wednesday that the manager of the Comédie Mondaine had offered her a principal position in his company. Two hundred francs a month. Play every night; a new piece every week or nearly so. Rehearsal every afternoon except Sunday, when there is a matinée. And find your own toilettes! She refused it.

ARNOLD BENNETT *by Mrs. Arnold Bennett*

He once gave an evening in his flat at which French poets, composers, and artists were present. I recited a few poems, most of which at the time were ultra modern, the work of Charles Baudelaire, Paul Verlaine, Albert Samain, Mallarmé.
This was a triumph for me . . . I felt that I had at last *le pied à l'étrier*. Soon, however, fate directed me into another path. I gave up the hope of a dramatic career to become the wife of the man I loved.

This is the first mention of those poetry recitals which were her unique medium of self-expression and which were later to play an important part in her married life.
Early in February he left Paris to join Eden Phillpotts at San Remo. Today, Eden Phillpotts's *The Farmer's Wife* is still in demand with amateur dramatic societies but then he was known only as a novelist writing about Devonshire. Arnold went to collaborate with him in a thriller subsequently called *The Statue*. It is also possible that Arnold went to think about his new relationship uninfluenced by the party concerned.
Arnold had a phobia about punctuality—or as Marguérite affirmed about not being unpunctual—and the following incident took place. It is taken from the second of the sketches she made of her husband who, when it came out in 1931, was beyond being infuriated by it as he had been by the first.

Extract from Marguérite's MY ARNOLD BENNETT

He claimed one day, in front of some friends and myself, that no woman could be punctual, and that few men could be. He went on : 'I would not dream, for instance, of asking any of my friends to see me off when I go to Italy. They would be sure to be late. Besides who would care to go to the Gare de Lyon at

22

eight in the morning, at this time of year?—except those catching the train . . .

Three days later the train to Italy was formed when I arrived at the station. I did not see the man I was looking for . . . I did not care to try to find him. He was sure to see me in time. If he did not see me I would not mind; I would go back home, after his train had left, and say nothing to anybody about my morning's failure. But Mr. Arnold Bennett was not a man to miss his train. He was not a man to rush at the last minute, to leave things to chance. I now could see him advancing, wearing a thick coat, a cap and thick gloves. He carried newspapers under his arm, and he came towards me smiling, as a Frenchman would have done. He said, 'You have come, and in good time. I would never have believed it possible.'

Postcard

Mademoiselle Marguérite Solié,
5 rue Guèrsant,   Nice
Paris XVIIe.   2nd February, 1907

I had a very good journey yesterday; the train was quite prompt, and my friend came to meet me at the station. I send you many kisses, and I shall write in a day or two. It was very nice of you to come to the station.

Your
Nold (A.B.)

Then comes the following crucial letter when he had had time to think things over. The letter from Marguérite to which it is a reply is lost but obviously she had opened her heart to him.

Mlle Marguérite Solié,   Hotel Royal,
5 rue Guèrsant,   San Remo, Italy.
Paris, XVIIe.   15th Feb. 1907
                                                              Friday night

My dearest girl,
I appreciate your letter very much indeed. I have never asked

23

you about your private life because I did not think it discreet to do so; but more because, whatever your private life was, my ideas about you would not have been affected by it. You see, I am a novelist, and a good judge of character; and I very soon saw that you had a good heart and were very sympathetic; that's always the essential thing. As you have been frank with me, I will be frank with you.

I earn a pretty good income, about 20,000 francs a year, but I have to pay a certain sum to my mother and one of my sisters, and I am afraid I shall soon have to find a lot of money for my other sister who wants a divorce from her husband. I have also spent a great deal of money on my flat, and my tastes generally are expensive. If I asked you to '*lâcher*' the 200 francs which you have, I should consider myself entirely responsible for you, and I do not feel justified in doing this in my present circumstance. If I had more money, and if I had not to think of my family, I should urge you to place yourself entirely under my protection. And I hope, one day, to be able to do this. But I will not do it now. You are able to judge by this time what my character is, and so I will not tell you anything, except that I am absolutely reliable, and to be trusted.

Let me give you 200 francs a month for your clothes. That will help you a little. And few things give me more pleasure than pretty clothes on a woman who knows how to dress. If you are free to change your flat, will you change it? But I do not want you to run any risks. I will pay the expenses of the removal, of course.

I myself always act slowly. But I really do think that we should agree very well. I like you very much, and I think I should like you more and more. And probably you would have no cause to regret being my friend. But I always keep my promises and therefore I do not make any promises that I am not quite sure of being able to keep.

Have you understood what I have said in English? I love you very much, darling, but I am a distinct type, very reflective, very egotistical, very prudent, very uncomplicated, and, with all this, absolutely sure of myself. Whoever does anything with me can count on me and on my fidelity and frankness. I kiss you on the lips. You are a woman of rare temperament, and you please me infinitely. I wait for your letter.

Thy Nold.

P.S. Work goes well. Let me tell you something. I began with 100 francs a month and nobody has helped me. One of these days I shall have plenty of cake.

Arnold's Journal—Friday, 19th April, 1907—Les Sablons

I came down here with Marguérite S on Tuesday, and I stay till next Monday. *Voilà une affaire qui me plaît infiniment!*

Arnold's Journal—Wednesday, 24th April, 1907—Les Sablons

Marguérite was telling me the other day her feelings when she lost her protector (*i.e. the law student*). How she saw nothing but the path in the cemetery for months. How his family left her to starve, giving her, after a long delay, 2,000 francs. How other women came to her and instead of sympathizing said : 'You must expect to lose your lover. That might happen to anyone. Why not you?' etc. And how they were secretly vexed when she retained her chic and got on to her feet again. Such was her account.

THE MERRY WIVES OF WESTMINSTER—*Ch. XI, by Mrs. Belloc Lowndes*

During one of my working visits to Paris I was asked by an English friend to an afternoon party, and I at once noticed a peculiar-looking man with a stocky figure, and a plain, somewhat fleshy, face. I felt deeply interested, a few moments later, to learn he was Arnold Bennett. At that time Bennett's stutter was far worse than it became in later life, but when he sat down the stutter became markedly less . . . When I had gone back to London after our first meeting, he began writing letters in which he told me all about his work. Then followed some weeks of silence, broken at last by a statement that he had been very ill with typhoid—the curse then, as I fear it is still, of all large French towns. He further wrote that he had been devotedly nursed by a French lady.

Arnold's Journal—Friday, 3rd May, 1907—Les Sablons

Then, at midnight, return of sanguinary diarrhoea. Ill in bed till Wednesday, under the doctor Bouteron. I was up all day yesterday; but today my intestines not being free altogether, and it being necessary that castor oil should procure their freedom, I am again in bed. Marguérite nursed me all the time, and not once has that creature (who is clearly a born nurse) made a gesture or used a tone that grated on my nerves. This is one of the most wonderful things that ever happened to me. Yesterday I wrote my first *chronique* for the *Evening News*.

Arnold's Journal—Tuesday, 7th May, 1907—Les Sablons

Marguérite departed yesterday, after three weeks, including my illness. I felt like a widower; and that ten years would elapse before Wednesday.

Les Sablons, incidentally, was a country retreat he had found at Fontainebleau, in the house of an old couple called Lebert.

Arnold's Journal—Saturday, 11th May, 1907—Les Sablons

I came down to Les Sablons with Marguérite on the following afternoon. The weather is hot and gorgeous. If I had simple, narrow tastes, what an ideal existence I could live down here with this ideal mistress! But I have all kinds of tastes that I can't satisfy here. And yet here I have now a beautiful little flat, a piano, music, books, electric light, a lovely garden, lovely scenery, quite extraordinarily good food; and I am looked after to admiration.

Arnold's Journal—Monday, 27th May, 1907—Paris

The effect of glitter and show on women. M. went to the concert very tired, with a headache, but beautifully dressed. She sat in an uncomfortable chair for over three hours, and emerged quite restored to health, and fresh and gay. She came home and ate 'petits fours' in bed because she was so hungry.

One thing she said the other day rather surprised me: 'Now that I belong absolutely to you, and my decision is final, and I am full of happiness and security, still I feel a little sad. I do not regret my decision—very far from that—but it seems to me that my life is over. I have nothing else to look forward to. All so arranged and finished.' This is exactly the sentiment that men have on the morrow of even a happy marriage: but I had not suspected that women felt it sufficiently to mention it.

Arnold's Journal—Tuesday, 4th June, 1907—Paris

On Friday last I decided I would marry M. That is to say I openly decided. I had decided, without admitting to myself that I had done so, several days before. I woke up at 3.0 a.m. on Saturday morning and I could not go to sleep again. And I had a continuous nervous headache, and very little sleep, until last night. Such is the result, in a highly nervous organisation, of betrothing yourself. I came down to Les Sablons on Saturday, and wrote to most of my friends on Sunday. I wrote an *Evening News* article on Sunday afternoon. But yesterday I did nothing. Today I wrote the eighth instalment of a humorous novel (i.e. *Buried Alive*) 4,000 words exactly, at a tremendous pace. I don't think I was actually writing more than four hours.

CHAPTER III

The Marriage

In an unpublished article dated September 1936, Marguérite has this to say about the reason for the marriage:

As for the 'illness through which I nursed him' it amounts to this:

On calling at his house one morning in the early summer of 1907, I was told by the maid that her master was in bed, seriously unwell. Josephine (*the maid*) being totally incompetent and the patient helpless, I took charge of him and soon ascertained that he was suffering from an acute attack of enteritis which had been brought about by a meal of which 'chou farci' was one of the chief courses. M. Emile Martin, who had shared in the repast as well as Dr. Bouteron who had been called in, confirmed the diagnosis. Within a few days the patient was quite well again. I leave it to the biographers of the future to decide whether when he asked me to become his wife, Arnold Bennett was suffering from a broken heart or an overdose of stuffed cabbage.

But this I know. He did not marry me just because he happened to want a wife (he had many women admirers); he did not marry me out of spite just because another woman had chucked him; he did not marry me just because I nursed him through an attack of indigestion. He married me with his eyes open and of his own free choice. He was no bashful lover, no victim of mooncalf love. He was an experienced bachelor of forty. He married me because I suited him.

He had said: 'I have spoken about you with my friends. All say that I should be right to marry you. So, then, would you be my wife?'

One of these friends was Emile Martin, a wealthy English-speaking Parisian, of whom Marguérite said in reminiscence that he had an influence over Arnold of which even Arnold himself was not aware. Martin had told him : She'd take you with her eyes shut'. What she replied to the proposal in fact will never be known but what she *said* she replied (in the *Resumé*) was : 'My poor friend, what on earth are you saying? Don't you know you will never be happy with me? I am so very French and you are so very English.' But she was argued into it and accepted.

With the French in 1907 the civil marriage of a national to a foreigner called for certificates of birth, of health, and of legal ability to marry; certificates from surviving parents and from the foreigner himself attested by an independent French national. As well, banns had to be published in the usual way.

As a native, Marguérite would be likely to know the ropes better than he, so he gave her into the care of an English lawyer called Bodington and left for England. He had contacts to renew in London, but more pressing was research into the background of the projected *Old Wives' Tale* which could only be undertaken in the Potteries and Manchester. It was the first (the second, if we are to count the visit to Menton) of his many desertions.

Mlle. M. Solié,   Sunday, 1907
5 rue Guersant,
Paris XVII.   London.

Chérie,
    The butter was a happy idea. I ate it all. Before eating it I took a couple of naps, and another afterwards. After the third nap, I made a second meal of what remained in my teeth. It was blowing horribly and, although the sea was marvellously bright with sun, no part of it bigger than a 20-centime piece was smooth. I was discreetly and decently ill. So there went the lunch you made me eat! I haven't been ill crossing the Channel for several years. Arrived at Dover, I found myself perfectly well and had a cup of tea and a sandwich, and a fourth nap. I am writing this in the train which is swift and rackety. It wearies me to death. In fifteen minutes I shall be in London.

All my love,
Noliton.

Mlle. M. Solié,   Golden Cross Hotel,
5 rue Guersant,   Charing Cross,
Paris XVII.   London.
                                         Monday, 1907
Chérie,

A revolution in my daily habits today! I dressed before
having tea. I got dressed alone, without you, which took a long
time. I can't dress quickly without interruptions. I must have
interruptions. The 'excuse me—may I come in?', 'excuse me,
would you fasten me up?', 'excuse me, where did you put the
etc., etc.' I was an hour over it this morning. Then I went down-
stairs to take my tea majestically in the restaurant of the hotel
with all the English papers to read. I like to have my tea like
that, surrounded by good waiters who know me and have
humoured me for many years. Having drunk my tea with great
ceremony, I have come into the lounge to write you a little note.
It's fresh but fine. I found my sister (Tertia) in very good shape.
Yesterday for the first time she got up for a few minutes (following the birth of her first daughter, Mary). But there is only
one topic of conversation. *It is you.* I met several friends
yesterday evening. They asked me what gewgaws you would
like as wedding presents! And so on. London is thronged with
people but lacks one person. What did she do yesterday? Let
her not forget her engagement . . .

Mlle. M. Solié,   Golden Cross Hotel,
5 rue Guersant,   Charing Cross.
Paris XVII.   London.
                                         Tuesday, 1907
My dearest child,

. . . I have had a letter from Bodington. He says he *thinks*
the first publication (of the banns) can be made next Sunday.
I hope there will be no doubt about it, and that you will manage
to let him have the consent of both your father and your mother
without any delay. If the marriage is postponed I shall be
extremely grieved.

I think I prefer to write to you in French as I always suspect
that you do not understand my English. Everyone wishes to
see you and I above all. I am horribly busy and a little run

down but I shall be better tomorrow. I took a little pill in the evening. Be of good cheer and give my respects to your mother. This isn't a letter but only a little nothing to remind you of my existence and that I love you.

Mlle. M. Solié,   Golden Cross Hotel,
5 rue Guersant,   Charing Cross.
Paris XVII.   London.
            Wednesday, 1907

Ma très chère Guite,

. . . I am not one of those miserable people who tell you how they are so terribly busy and preoccupied with the things of the greatest importance that they cannot find time to write postcards. Me, I am very busy and preoccupied, but the thing of the greatest importance that I have to do is write to you every day, and this I am doing . . .

I understand perfectly well how bored you are, and that your mother gets on your nerves. I seriously assure you that every moment I am by myself I am enormously bored. I would infinitely prefer to be with you in Paris. And I am disgusted that there are still fifteen days to wait before I get married. I beg you, don't neglect anything in this business. If it's more sure to go to Mans, go there. And when the papers have been signed make certain at once with Bodington that they are in order. Make all the arrangements and ask Bodington the next time you see him if he will send a clerk or someone conversant with these things to go with me to the Mairie for the ceremony so that I shan't suffer any embarrassments. I can face unavoidable embarrassments with calm, but embarrassments which are avoidable—I can face those with calm, too, but the calm is false and lacks sincerity.

Mlle. M. Solié,   Golden Cross Hotel,
5 rue Guersant,   Charing Cross,
Paris XVII.   London.
         Thursday morning, 1907

Chérie,

I received your letter yesterday evening. Regarding your

mother you have all my sympathy. I know her! But it is necessary to put up with her. I infinitely regret that you are sad. I
wish I could put my arms round you so as to give you back
forthwith a gay and smiling face. It worries me enormously
when I think that you are bothered like that all alone in Paris.
I had the mad idea of rushing back to Paris to tell you that I
am always here and that all goes well, and that a fortnight is
nothing. It will pass like the éclair I am eating. As for London,
I am beginning to have enough of it. What a day yesterday!
. . . At six o'clock I went to my sister's (Tertia) where I dined.
I had already given her your salutations, etc., and she charged
me with some truly kind things to say to you. She's a splendid
woman. She is extremely impatient to make your acquaintance.
She almost persuaded me to bring you to London immediately
after the marriage. But I refused . . . Tomorrow I shall go to
mother's. You were right not to go to the photographer's if you
didn't feel up to it. Sweetheart, don't worry. Don't get angry
with your mother. In only a little time we shall be together
again, and all will be well. Ah! What a pity that I am not more
demonstrative so that I could convince you how perfectly
indispensable you are to me, and how tender I am, at heart!
I embrace you tenderly, my sweet Guite.

Mlle. M. Solié,   Golden Cross Hotel,
5 rue Guersant,   Charing Cross,
Paris XVII.   London.
                                              Friday, 1907

Chérie,
    . . . This stay in London begins to weary me. I have had my
fill of it. I am exhausted. Absolutely! Happily my small visits
are all done with . . . At heart I am bored here . . . Bustle the
lawyers up, as much as you can. I know those imbeciles. They
make a heap out of nothing, and take four days sitting on their
bottoms without laying an egg, so to speak. Make sure the
banns will be published on Sunday. If they are not published
I shall assassinate Bodington; then they will guillotine me and
there won't be any marriage. So you see where your interest
lies! God, how I want to rest in the arms of someone who knows

how to coddle me! In your absence, it must be my mother. Poor woman, she's not very experienced in that kind of thing. Sweet, I infinitely regret that you are bored. You have something to busy yourself with, all the same. I wait impatiently to see you in your new dresses and finery. Here, there's a terrible wind, but what does that matter? The weather means nothing to me. Think of me, and remain beautiful against my return.

Thy Nold.

p.s. Yes, you should give the room to Joséphine, since you ask for my advice. I am asked for articles. I know that's no concern of yours, but do you want me to write them? I absolutely insist that if you worry me about Joséphine and her sisters, you worry yourself with writing my articles.

Mlle. M. Solié,	179 Waterloo Road,
5 rue Guersant,	Burslem,
Paris XVIII.	Stoke-on-Trent.

Saturday, June, 1907

Chérie,

Your letter to hand this morning gave me much pleasure. I do hope that the arrangements for the consents continue to go well. I fear that there will be a delay at Brest. In any case, I shall be uneasy until the moment we leave the Mairie. Your messages for my mother gave her enormous pleasure. It's astonishing how (such) messages charm. Ah, my dearest, what a *fusillade* of questions about you broke out when I arrived! They were like a hailstorm . . . You don't say anything about your health. I suppose it must be well. We are going to be happy in a quite particular way. I am sure. We understand one another. Mother is already pleased with you. She sends you kindnesses of all sorts, my sister (Sissie) also. When you come here you will have some rather tiresome experiences, in this filthy factory region. Sweetheart, I embrace you in my own way, and I leave you. Be sure that I am well, and that in my heart I am infinitely bored.

Nold.

33

Mlle. M. Solié,   179 Waterloo Road,
5 rue Guersant,   Burslem,
Paris XVII.   Stoke-on-Trent.
                                            Sunday, 1907
Ma chérie,

I have been very busy today. I was obliged to write a long article. And the moment has come when I must go to my brother's (Frank's) for dinner. It's very frustrating, all this fuss about the publication of banns. Under cover I am sending you a small cheque, which you can draw on when you have need. I wait impatiently for tomorrow's letter to learn if you have succeeded with the banns. If they aren't published, I shall make my arrangements forthwith. Bodington cannot 'do impossibilities' but he should have known that my presence at the Mairie was necessary. He told me, on the contrary, quite clearly, that he could do without me. And with that I came to England.

Anyway, all that—it's nothing. All will be well. Everything will sort itself out. I am tired. The day will come when I shall no longer be tired. We shall be together. We shall be married. And we shall love each other forever. Your letters are my joy, in the morning or in the evening. I don't cry but I am very moved. It's horribly cold here. I am very busy. Mother waits for me. She sends you a thousand messages. Kiss me, and I kiss your ears.

Thy Noliton.

P.S. You must put your signature on the back of the cheque.

Mlle. M. Solié   179 Waterloo Road,
5 rue Guersant,   Burslem,
Paris XVII.   Stoke-on-Trent.
                                      Monday morning, 1907
Dearest,

I received your letter this morning and I am very pleased with it. Write forthwith to my mother. She will be very touched. When I give her your respects etc. every morning she is infinitely pleased.

I do hope that everything for the marriage is now in order.

34

If you are not quite sure, please go to Bodington at once, and make sure. And tell *them* to telegraph me if things are not in order. If I hear nothing I shall assume that all is right.

It seems about ten years since I left you. But, really, it is only 8 days. I shall certainly return to Paris and to Marguérite not later than *Monday* next. I shall arrive late in the evening.

I have written to the dealer, bullying him. About the electric kettle, yes, I think you may write and tell them to send it, and I will pay the thirty francs.

Don't forget the wedding ring.

I am going to Manchester tomorrow with my brother (Frank) and sister-in-law (Florence) to buy cutlery and any old silver I can find in a shop which makes a speciality of such things. My mother will buy the servants' aprons. But I think we will get the table-cloths in Paris. I have ordered my alpaca jacket. It is superb. I am also buying a white hat which is absolutely the *dernier cri* of chic. Also neckties, very striking. The weather is very bad. Rainy and cold, all the time. But my health is good and *I am sleeping well.*

Sweetheart, I am like you. I long terribly to be with you. It disgusts me to be separated. It seems idiotic and offensive to be so far from you. And so I am profoundly depressed. BUT I AM PHILOSOPHIC.

The great philosophers always knew how to embrace their wives. And I embrace you with the tenderness and warmth of the greatest.

Noliton.

Mlle. M. Solié,   179 Waterloo Road,
5 rue Guersant,   Burslem,
Paris XVII.   Stoke-on-Trent.
                                     Wednesday, 1907

Chérie,

I am glad the bans are published. But what carelessness on Bodington's or the solicitor's part that your mother's certificate had to be redrawn! In all my life I have known nothing but evil in solicitors and attorneys, and I have always found that breed careless, idiotic, inexact, and laughable, even though often very polite. I am sorry, my child, that you suffer. It will pass...

Mlle. M. Solié,   179 Waterloo Road,
5 rue Guersant,   Burslem,
Paris XVII.   Stoke-on-Trent.
                                                      Wednesday, 1907
Chérie,
  ... We went to Manchester yesterday. At this moment we (that is to say you and I) possess silverware and a very nice cutlery set. You have saltcellars, pepper-pots, containers for sugar, for fruit, for fish, in short everything necessary to a household. Oue of my brothers-in-law (Frank Beardmore) has given me a vase and a large, exquisite, dazzling faience bowl. Mother goes out this morning to buy aprons and caps (white bonnets) for the maid. I shall be pretty encumbered with luggage ... I sleep like you, with perfect expertise. All at once I have become one of the most accomplished sleepers in the entire world. I thought of making myself a professor of sleep, and giving lectures. All because I smoke plenty of good cigars! The weather is nobody's business. It's terrible. Cold to make you perish, and rain, rain, rain, endlessly.
                 Sweetheart, a long, tender kiss.
                          Your Noliton
P.S. Mother sends you her greetings and thanks you very sincerely. She is much, much better. My other relations, too, send you a thousand kind thoughts.

Mlle. M. Solié,   179 Waterloo Road,
5 rue Guersant,   Burslem.
Paris XVII.   [undated]

Darling,
  I shall return on Friday evening. I have received an idiotic letter from Bodington who asks me for a Foreigner's Declaration for Saturday. I have not the least idea what this is, a Foreigner's Declaration. So, I shall be coming to find out, in time. He wearies me to death, does Bodington.

I don't know what time the train arrives, but it will be at the Gare du Nord. The train leaves Charing Cross, London, at 2.20 in the afternoon. You will find it in the Chaix time-table in my desk.

Bodington wearies me to death, but all the same I am very happy to be coming back the sooner.

Thy
Noliton.

Arnold's Journal—Friday, 5th July 1907

Yesterday, at 11 a.m. at the Mairie of the 9th Arrondissement, Paris, I was married to Marie Marguérite Soulié, commonly known as Solié.

Frederick Marriott, from whose reminiscence of Arnold[1] the following extract is taken, played a special role in Arnold's life in that it was at the Marriotts' house in Chelsea, soon after Arnold's arrival in London, that he was first introduced into the society of artists. More, it was there that Arnold began the slow reshaping of himself from a raw provincial youth into an acceptable man of letters. (It is questionable whether he succeeded : twenty years later G. K. Chesterton was unkindly describing him as someone who'd come up for the Cup and failed to go back.) A small, merry, twinkling man, an inveterate practical joker, Marriott was Head of the Art Department at Goldsmith's College, London.

I wrote to him at once, suggesting that in consequence of his recent mariage he might like us to put off our visit till a later date. His reply, written on a postcard, was characteristically brief. It read, 'Dear Frederick, I shall need you all the more. A.B.' Thus it came about that we spent one of the most delightful holidays possible, and were introduced to a very beautiful and romantic region of France (Les Sablons) only forty miles distant from Paris.

When the cab drew up to the door of the house, Mrs. Bennett

---

[1] *My Association with Arnold Bennett,* Keele University Library's Occasional Publication No. 3, 1967.

met us radiant and smiling, and with a short halt between each word said, 'How do you do, will you take tea with me?', an opening evidently previously rehearsed. Our subsequent interchange of broken English and broken French, supported by expressive gesticulations to cover our deficiencies, was productive of much merriment between us during our time there, and on many other occasions. She was a tall, graceful, and strikingly handsome woman, and she had excellent taste in dress. Moreover, she had the gift of wearing fine clothes with the best effect.

Marguérite's Journal
Today is the anniversary of our marriage which took place in Paris—with no honeymoon. Only a few days after, we left Paris for 'Les Sablons' near Fontainebleau where Arnold had a studio. Mr. and Mrs. Marriott joined us and stayed for a long holiday—six weeks. My husband at that time was very fond of cycling. So as to please him, and so as to avoid being left often on my own, I decided to learn to ride a bicycle. My husband bought a very nice one for me and soon I could join the three of them for a short outing. Then A.B. organised a long tour in the district—it was to take us the whole day. Before we started I had to point out that, as I was not very experienced and unable to stand too many long miles of the journey, I would like to take the train. However, the first day I cycled like the others just to please Arnold, despite the weariness it meant for me. I thus rode a distance of 75 kilometres. I was dead tired when we got to our hotel, but the next day we had to start at 6.0 in the morning. I had to do 65 kilometres that day like the others. I was absolutely worn out and was too tired even to eat. The same thing happened two months later when the Marriotts had gone back to London, when, to please A.B., we started out for a few days ourselves. Once again A.B.'s programme had to be fulfilled and as a result I fainted on the way. It was the beginning of a very serious nervous breakdown.

This episode of the bicycles irresistibly brings to mind one of the great predictive incidents in literature, when Anna Karenina's lover, Vronsky, rides to death his mare Frou-frou.

CHAPTER IV

One Of The Family

MY ARNOLD BENNETT *by Marguérite*

One of his sisters (Tertia) at first terrified me. When I first saw her I kissed her, but she was not to be kissed so impulsively, not even by her French sister-in-law. No. She stood straight, smiling, but on her guard, and looked severe. It paralysed me. I blushed as if I had committed a crime.

Sympathetic as my husband was, he had no patience with those who could not keep their emotions to themselves. I was, at the time, under the delusion that one could always let oneself go with one's better half—but apparently no two people can be really themselves with each other. Certainly in the Five Towns, in Arnold's time, they were not trained to have perfect confidence, even in the chosen one. A great French writer has said and written *'Chaque anglaise est une île'*.

My sister-in-law was an island.

He was proud and very excited when he introduced me to his mother. He first took off his hat—apparently quite calm— and then his coat, in the hall, while his mother, in the sitting-room close by, also waited calmly till the maid opened the door.

'Hello, Mater! Here she is,' said her son, pushing me into the room.

I did not kiss her; my experience with her daughter living in London prevented me. She kissed me. She said little. She did not smile. She looked at me. She knew a lot about my everyday doings. Marguérite's dresses, headaches, walks, dogs, were inexhaustible daily sources for him to draw copy from.

Now the Mater saw me for the first time in the flesh, she being very small thought me very tall, taller than I really was. She thought I looked well.

She poured out tea for us. I perceived she and her son did not talk much, and certainly there was no manifestation of joy. I understood little of what they said.

I remember her that morning in her sittingroom where

breakfast had been served. She was in black as usual, looking, as always, handsome and sweet, stiff and straight. She wore her usual expression which was in reality a mask behind which was hidden whatever thoughts and feelings might pass through her consciousness. She had a natural expression which was neither repellent nor attractive. It made me feel self-conscious as well as matter-of-fact, and I longed to go back to France where we were to settle in Fontainebleau.

The Mater was not sure that I understood her when she addressed me. That morning she wanted to make sure I should understand what she had to say, to me in particular, before we departed. Arnold having left us, she asked what I thought of my visit to the district. I do not know if she understood my answer.

'We haven't seen much of him, have we? You are to have him always. I am pleased he has got you. I may die in peace now. Remember that if at any time you don't get on I shall know it is not your fault.'

In Burslem, a closely knit and often interrelated community whose families had lived in the district for generations and packed the local churchyards with their dead, the Bennetts, it must be admitted, were looked upon as *parvenus*. Enoch Bennett had come up from nothing; he had been a pawnbroker and a bankrupt; he still owned very little, and he had put up his solicitor's plate over the hill in another town—in Hanley, that is.

The one exception in the public regard was Arnold's mother, Sarah Ann, whose family owned the draper's business in St. John's Square, which is portrayed in *The Old Wives' Tale*. She happened to be humourless but she was everywhere accepted and loved. (Indeed, her memory is still loved by those who knew her.) She had supported her terrifying husband through his lean years by serving in her father's shop, and a family legend tells how she was found trimming a hat while teaching the formidable brood at her feet their alphabet.

Following her husband's death in 1902, as though during all those years of servitude she had secretly been planning for the moment, she became gay and independent.

Rather from knowledge of my grandmother[1] than from

[1] The "I" in editorial comments, here and subsequently, refers to George Beardmore.

Marguérite's reportage of the incident, I should say that 'the Mater's' final remarks, above quoted, are very probably true.

Because on that occasion Marguérite went with him there are necessarily no letters, but two years later, when he made a similar journey to research for *Clayhanger,* she was to follow him to Burslem. By that time they had settled in a house of their own, the Villa des Néfliers, at Avon-Fontainebleau, where, in July, 1908, he had finished *The Old Wives' Tale.* One imagines that Marguérite was staying in Paris before crossing to England and joining him.

Mme. Bennett,
Hotel de Londres et New York,   Burslem,
Paris   Tuesday, 1st December, 1909

Chérissime,

Here I am. It rains unceasingly. The thermometer beside the bed stood at 5 degrees. I occupy the big room. Everyone asks where you are. Florence (Frank Bennett's wife) has already fixed up an entire programme for your week here. You are engaged every evening. Mother is well enough. This morning at breakfast she cried while telling me that Frank didn't want to buy what coal is necessary. But she's well enough. I eat at Frank's. With mother, father, and the children. One of the children is in bed. I went to see him. Richard (*Frank Bennett's eldest son*) would very much like to come and visit us . . . I have everywhere told the story of the loss of your umbrella. Everyone is very sympathetic. Everyone wishes to see you. I hope that you had a good lunch with Ida[2], that the umbrella has been found, and that you are not on bad terms with the manageress of the hotel. A heap of letters is waiting for me. In brief, I am enormously busy . . .

Mme. Bennett,   179 Waterloo Road,
Hotel de Londres et New York,   Burslem, Stoke-on-Trent.
Paris   Thursday, 2nd December, 1909

Dearest Child,

It's a good thing you aren't here. The weather surpasses that

[2] Godebski, wife of Cepa Godebski, a painter.

of Switzerland. It is not cold, but it is barbaric—thick rain and furious wind. I went to a public dinner last night and ate nothing but turkey and soup, and a little sweet jelly. Consequence : I was quite well this morning. I slept till 5 o'clock. Unfortunately breakfast is not till 8.30 o'clock. Florence's youngest child (*Vernon Bennett*) and Sissie's youngest child (*George Beardmore*) are both ill in bed. The Mater is much better, but has a cold. It is not surprising. She lights the gas-stove in my room each night, but not her own ! ! And she is nearly 70. I am still constipated ! ! ! If I don't go within half an hour I shall shoot it out with my revolver . . . I have refused to make any speeches at all while you are here, because they make *you* so nervous. But last night the municipal councillors much insisted that I should make a speech to the students in the Town Hall next week but one. I wrote today declining. I have not yet heard from you, or from your umbrella. Well, I embrace you in my Arnoldique way.

A.

Madame Arnold Bennett,   Midland Hotel,
c/o W. W. Kennerley Esq.,   Manchester.
37 Clarendon Road, Putney.   4th December, 1909.
Friday evening. 10½ hours.

Chérissime,

. . . I am very glad that you are not coming to England today. The crossing would have been terrible. But I suppose that there has been just as much rain and wind in Paris as here. It was an extraordinarily rough night, and today it has rained and snowed and hailed all day. It was still raining when I came to Manchester this morning. I was given an absolutely astounding welcome by the managers of the Manchester paper. All of them are singularly clever people, nice, and charming. No less than four of them offered me lunch in the most stylish hotel outside London. Then they gave me the freedom of their majestic boardrooms etc. They arranged for me to see all the numbers of the years 1872 to 1882 which I need for my novel . . .

You will get this letter upon your arrival in London. I fear that the crossing will have been very bad and you ill. However,

42

you will be all right at Tertia's. I return to Burslem tomorrow for lunch. Briefly, and in short, I love you, and am anxious to see you again.

Thy A.B. husband.

Mme. Arnold Bennett,
c/o W. W. Kennerley Esq.,
Putney.

179 Waterloo Road,
Burslem.
Sunday, 5th December, 1909

Chérissime,

I am happy that you have arrived. When I read your last letter, in which you told me the story of the 'Marriage of Figaro' without lunch, I wasn't at all happy. I told myself, so that's this woman when she's left on her own! She goes to the theatre without lunch. Yes, yes, I know that you had headaches, and I am sorry, but you ought to have taken something. I imagine that the journey, although awful, will have done your headaches etc. good. I was afraid that you would arrive here worn out and half dead, and when I saw your handwriting on the envelope when I came down this morning, it relieved me. It seems to me that you came out of that journey very well.

It would be infinitely sweet of you to go on Monday morning and see Jessie Farrar (*possibly a daughter of Dr. John Farrar, of Putney*) on my behalf. I made all arrangements with her, quite clearly, to have the typing of the play here this morning, Sunday, without fail. It hasn't come. Would you ask her if she sent it off, and how. The thing is urgent. I shall be waiting for it tomorrow morning, certain, and I am asking you to do this only as a precaution. If it's the fault of the post, so much the worse; but if Jessie hasn't sent it off, she is to blame, because she promised me that she would.

I went to bed (in Manchester) at two o'clock, Friday evening (which is to say, Saturday morning). I slept till 10 o'clock, my child! I caught the midday train to get back here. Sissie's baby is *very ill*; so Sissie and Frank (Beardmore) didn't come here yesterday evening as had been arranged. I asked Dr. Russell to come, and we finished the evening at Frank (Bennett's) at one o'clock. I slept well and am well . . .

43

I can tell you that I await Friday with impatience.
I embrace you tenderly, dear wife.

Thy A.B.

Mme. Bennett,   179 Waterloo Road,
c/o W. W. Kennerley Esq.,   Burslem, Stoke-on-Trent.
Putney.   Monday, 6th December, 1909

Chérissime,

. . . The Mater was unwell yesterday morning but today
she is better. You will excuse me if I write a perfectly silly letter
but my head is so boiling with politics and opera and as well
with all the odd things I am continually gathering together
for my book, that I can't write a letter suitable for my poor
child . . .

The typing for the play has arrived.

My love to everyone.

Thy A.

Mme. Bennett,   179 Waterloo Road,
c/o W. W. Kennerley Esq.,   Burslem, Stoke-on-Trent.
Putney.   Tuesday, 7th December, 1909

Ma sposa carissima,

. . . Florence wants you to take the twelve-fifteen train, on
Friday. You will arrive here at $3\frac{1}{2}$ o'clock. Any train after that
will be too late because of Frank's rehearsals, which means
that we don't sit down to a meal until six o'clock or half-past.
All the talk here is about next week's performances (*of 'Carmen'*,
an amateur operatic production). I shall dine with several pals
at Dr. Russell's tomorrow evening. No women. He invites you
to supper after the performance on Monday next. He is insisting,
and I have accepted on your behalf . . .

Mme. Bennett,   179 Waterloo Road,
c/o W. W. Kennerley Esq.,   Burslem, Stoke-on-Trent.
Putney.   Wednesday, 8th December, 1909

Chérissime,

I had your long and excellent letter this morning. I shall be at Stoke on Friday. So will Florence. I slept very badly last night, but I am very well. It is unarguable that alone I don't know what to do with myself . . .

Mme. Bennett,   179 Waterloo Road,
c/o W. W. Kennerley Esq.,   Burslem, Stoke-on-Trent.
Putney.   Thursday, 9th December, 1909

I have just read your long letter. I reply at once (9.30) because this afternoon I shall be much occupied. My throat is sore but it's a bit better this morning. I slept well. My overcoat will delight you. It would be a mistake not to bring your best dress —not so as to wear it but so as to show it to some of my relations. They are counting on you for that kind of thing. I advise you to bring it.

So, tomorrow, at 3.55, I shall be at Stoke station.

Enormously busy, with the novel and politics.

I embrace you tenderly, *ma svelte chatte.*

She visited the Potteries for the last time in 1955, when Arnold and his brothers and sisters were long since dead. It was a sentimental visit. She was received by the Lord Mayor, visited the Arnold Bennett Museum at 205, Waterloo Road, and asked the driver of the official car to stop a moment outside the gate of No. 179. She was eighty-one-years old.

CHAPTER V

Money and Kisses

ARNOLD BENNETT *by Marguérite*

I do not think it is indiscreet of me to repeat what he himself has said to many of his friends when they have happened to wonder why on earth he goes on working so hard when there is no apparent reason for doing so. 'My boy, you don't understand that the great thing which makes me go on writing and writing is simply that I must . . . I love work . . . I believe in work . . . the only thing worth living for . . . Apart from that, between you and me, if I had not heavy expenses to cope with I would not work quite so hard as I do . . . I love luxury, and luxury costs money . . . I could not work so hard if I did not know that my luxuries depended upon what I earn. I make plenty of money and I like spending it . . . I hate debts, and yet if I know that I owe money it makes me work harder than ever . . . I could not work if I did not have to see that my bank balance is on the right side. It would be a terrible catastrophe, my boy, just good enough for children . . . the children you and I are at times.

Between 1908 and 1911 no less than six novels[1] appeared in addition to *The Old Wives' Tale,* also five handbooks on the business of living (e.g. *The Human Machine, How to Live on 24 Hours a Day*); three plays were put on in London, and reviews were regularly appearing by him in *The New Age* under the pen-name of Jacob Tonson. Success was his, separating him from his wife rather like a horse bolting with its rider.

Henceforward he was perpetually on the move and writing to Marguérite rather like Marlborough manoeuvring armies round Europe and writing to Sarah; one is left wondering why, in Arnold's case, he didn't take her with him. Because she was ailing, or because she embarrassed him, or because he trusted only in himself? Often enough, as appears in the following extracts, he writes to her sometimes twice a day, sometimes when going about his affairs in the same city as she.

[1] *Buried Alive,* Chapman & Hall, 1908; *The Glimpse,* Chapman & Hall, 1909; *Clayhanger,* Methuen, 1910; *Helen with the High Hand,* Chapman & Hall, 1910; *The Card,* Methuen, 1911; *Hilda Lessways,* Methuen, 1911.

Burslem.
Sunday morning.
1911.

Very dear child,

. . . Thank you for your delicious letter which gave me intense pleasure by its unique turn of phrase. I did not write to you yesterday. It was useless because there is no post to London on Sundays. However, there is much to tell you. Yesterday I wrote a précis for the last book on *Hilda Lessways*. [*'Clayhanger', 'Hilda Lessways' and 'These Twain' form a trilogy. The Doran mentioned is George Doran, his American publisher, whose enthusiasm for 'The Old Wives' Tale' had largely contributed to its success.*] Doran wired to say that the paper in question is ready to abandon its usual rule, which prevents the purchase of a book of which the whole manuscript hasn't been read! So I sent him a précis of the last chapters, and there is a chance (a thin one) that they will take the outline of the unfinished Hilda for a price of 25000000000000000000 francs (I wish to convey two million) . . . Everyone asks for news of you. I had a good enough solitary journey from London. The tea-room at the station terminus was crowded with women. Not a table. I installed myself in the station bar, on a stool 1m. 75c. high, and I drank a cup of tea and ate a plate of chicken and ham. Cost—one and fivepence. I would much have liked the Godebskis to have seen me in that bar on that stool.

Burslem.
11th April, 1911.

Très chérie,

Your letter to hand. Very good. I don't doubt that the purse is lovely. It's clear that you don't find Putney too boring. Nor I either, here. But . . . As you say, I express myself badly . . . The contract with Doran for the humorous book [*The Card*] is completed. It guarantees me 17,500 francs for the outline and 12,500 for the book. In all, a minimum of 30,000 francs. Not bad for two months' work . . . Mother is well enough, but she is a terrible grumbler. The thing is, she's finished. One has to have enormous patience to live with her.

Authors' Club, London.
22nd April, 1911.

Très chère enfant,

Your letter gave me pleasure. Now! I will tell you something that will please you. I have re-read nearly all of what I have written of 'Hilda' and it is really good. Some pages are stunning. If only I can finish it in as brilliant a fashion!

So you were in London yesterday! I, too. Extremely. I lunched with (H.G.) Wells and someone else at the Reform Club—plentifully. Then I went to the photographer's. Idiotically I mistook the address. Gower Street instead of Baker Street. So, being late, I took a taxi . . . I met Rickards [*an artist and architect with whom, despite Rickard's Bohemian ways, Arnold had a long-standing friendship*] at the Café Royal in a horrible atmosphere. He was waiting for some friends who didn't turn up. Later, behold us at the Palace Music Hall to see the Russian ballet. Pavlova was really very good. The Galsworthys were there. Also a mulatto cocotte with whom Rickards actually sleeps! He says that she's very good and that her shoulders are a lovely colour. I told him that I had always longed to sleep with a negress. He offered me the mulatto girl. However, I didn't go along with the idea . . . I slept well until 8 o'clock. I felt tired but all right. All the morning I worked. I am very much the subject of conversation at this club. I am even its star. Every minute I surprise couples who whisper : 'He . . . *The Old Wives' Tale* . . . very good . . . very fine.' And when I draw near, they fall silent, embarrassed. In the *Manchester Guardian* this morning is the reproduction of the caricature (of me) by Max (Beerbohm).

The foregoing are representative of a series of letters—from the Hotel de Londres et New York in Paris, the Authors' Club in London, the *Guardian* offices in Manchester, Burslem, and from Glasgow, where his play *The Great Adventure*, an adaptation of the novel *Buried Alive*, was to be produced by a repertory company—in which he tells her of his affairs, always with the greatest affection.

In September of this year, 1911, she wrote the first letter that has survived.

Arnold Bennett Esq.,   Hotel de Londres et New York,
Glasgow.   Paris.
                                     19th September, 1911.

My love,

I was rejoicing at having placed John (a dog) in the hands of Gabrielle (*her sister*) and lo and behold this morning I had a letter from her explaining all the nuisance she had suffered because of it the very first day and all the nuisance she was likely to have, with the result—Come and collect your dog! So I am going. The far side of Passy. I thought at first of taking the dog to Fontainebleau, but that would be too much of a business. I am leaving tomorrow and have several small things to attend to. I am just wondering about taking it with me to England. I shall leave it in quarantine in Newhaven. That will be three months. Following that I would hope to find a charitable soul who will take care of it until our return to Cannes. Now I swear to you that after John I shan't have any more dogs. Poor beast!

Marvellous weather. I slept like a log. I have read 252 pages of *Hilda*. Some of the things in it are written with infinite tact. You can say anything because you know how to do it.

I am delighted that you have arrived at Glasgow for the première. Success must come! I am longing to hear the news of this première. I long also to be present at the première of HONEYMOON . . .

This hotel is filled with English and Americans. One of them has just come near me smoking a cigar. I swallowed the smoke and began to cough. It's horrible! Well! Now I am going to look for my dog. It's jolly. It's jollier that I kiss you. That I love you is happiness.

                            Thy Marguérite.

Early in the following month Arnold left her to sail for the States, a longer and much more rewarding excursion than any he had hitherto undertaken. In any study of the marriage, due attention must be paid to the fact that Marguérite did not go with him. Why? A hint is given that she may have thought herself pregnant, but this is no real reason. She suffered from headaches and may have been ailing but then one wonders why she suffered from headaches and why she was ailing when physically she was robust and lived to an advanced old age. Was the strain of living with a man so exceptional too much for her? In the family the belief was generally held that the marriage broke up because he did not share his life with her, did not take her to the States with him, but more probably the baffling situation had arisen in which husband and wife loved each other devotedly and yet could only be happy apart.

> on board the Cunard
> R.M.S. *Lusitania.*
> 7th October, 1911.

Dearest Girl,
    Immediately I got on this boat, I was struck by a new sense of my own importance. Seats at the purser's dining-table had been reserved for me, and deckchairs also. The Chairman of Cunard had given orders that I was to be looked after, and Mr. Hobley, the Liverpool manager, came and showed Knoblock[2] and me over the ship, and offered me another berth if I wanted it. I didn't . . .

> R.M.S. *Lusitania.*
> 7th October, 1911.

. . . What are you doing? I fear that you were very sad when you went back to our bedroom to pack up our things. I have not seen a single chic woman. I wish you were here to show them. You would be a sensation. Never mind. Though far away, I adore you still. I am now going to my solitary little bed. Much love, many kisses.

> Thy A.

> R.M.S. *Lusitania.*
> Wednesday, 11th October, 1911.

I embrace you, my cocotte. You will not understand the meaning of all this but I will tell you. I had the idea of sending you

---

[2] Arnold collaborated with Edward Knoblock in the play *Milestones,* which was first produced at the Royalty, London, in 1912.

some kisses by radio this morning. I thought of *three* kisses. I wrote out the telegram, and they said it would cost 26 shillings. I thought this rather dear, so you must take it that I sent 26 kisses at one shilling a piece . . . not too dear, I think.

George Doran's House,
New York.
20th October, 1911.

Dearest Girl,

It is very evident that you have made a profound impression on both the Dorans. Mrs. Doran talks of you all the time, and is extremely anxious to see you again. I am glad you are inviting people to Cedric's[3] concert. I hope you will do all this kind of thing very freely, and be generous in all ways, as we have heaps of money, and money is made (by me) to be spent generously by my wife. I am not spending much money here. I want when I come home, to go straight away to Cannes with you, alone, as soon as I can. We must spend two or three days in Paris. But as little as possible. What's necessary is you, and you, and you, and peace. Between caresses and talks and intimacies I have work to do. Now your letters and above all the endings of your letters have touched me very much. I can't finish a letter like you, but you understand me.

Thy A.

George Doran,
New York.
Sunday, 22nd October, 1911

Dearest Girl,

What I miss most (after you) is *people who understand art*. I also miss Paris tremendously. Where people understand life and talk about it freely. Here, nearly everything is puritanical —even the cocottes—as in London. But (the organisation of) business is perfect. To visit offices, to understand the organisation, and the organisation of business, is a real pleasure. I have a taste for business. As proof, no agent, neither here nor in London, not even the celebrated Pinker (his own agent), has

---

[3] Cedric Sharpe, a friend from Arnold's early years in London, had become the cellist of the day.

been able to get more than 62,500 francs for a précis. I have personally intervened. I direct it, I take the upper hand, I tell the others to be quiet, and I get 75,000 francs *for the American rights alone*. I tell you that I am proud of it, and I have written to Pinker accordingly.

George Doran,
New York.
26th October, 1911.

. . . I continue to make money without working for it. I had more than 1,500 francs this morning for nothing. I intend to give you another 1,000 as a supplementary present, and monthly you shall have what you wish. I don't like giving you presents because all I have is yours. You will *take* it as you please. It's just like that. And I embrace you and kiss you, and I love you as you love me.

Hotel Touraine,
Boston.
29th October, 1911.

Although I am enormously entertained, I have had enough of the United States, and what I need now is you, tranquillity, and France. Pinker has sold for 12 sous editions of two of my foulest sensational romances, making a total of 3,750 francs. More money! Also I have just arranged to write two *stories* in 1913 and two in 1914 for 20,000 francs the four. It's mad. They begged me. To get my things at that price they immorally threw themselves onto their knees.

I kiss you in a languorous and tender weariness, my little one.

Thy A.

George Doran,
New York.
Sunday, 5th November, 1911.

Dearest Girl,

I think always of the days when we shall be together. I see you in our very special little suite when we shall be together. I see you dressed and undressed. I see you in a new black nightgown which will at once make you everything that is Paris. Very fine, elegant, and sensual! I take you. I love you. I assault the said nightgown. Afterwards I watch you do all the little things you have to. I see you [*illegible*]. I would even like to see you when you are otherwise busy.

So you understand that you are for me, and that you are mine. I kiss you, my dearest child, and I would like to leave tomorrow to be with you. The few days we spend in Paris, we shall spend in a chic hotel because it will be a new honeymoon. Let's say the Hotel Meurice.

I kiss you tenderly,
Thy A.

8th November, 1911.

. . . Mme. Doran had invited some charming petticoats, M. Doran, and another gentleman, to tea at the Plaza Hotel, one of the chic hotels, the hotel to which we shall come when you visit here with me . . . In fact I am too much flattered and courted in this country. It's frightening. And in all the public places people look at me, because my picture is in all the papers, and I very much resemble my picture. Even the barbers say suddenly, in a particular tone of voice : 'Mr. Bennett', in a high voice so that everyone shall know who has just come in. When you come here you will be someone, I tell you. You will be the wife of an individual more celebrated than all the great individuals in the literary world. And everybody awaits you, with a sort of impatience, because I am always talking about you, and Mme. Doran never forgets to laud your charm.

The Bellevue Stratford,
Philadelphia.
Wednesday, 22nd November, 1911.

. . . I hope you will buy all the dresses and other things you wish and that you won't forget the dark nightdresses about which I wrote you. That's something I have always wanted, and that I have never seen. This time I hope to be gratified. Eight days and I shall be on board the *Lusitania*. Truly, that alone is what interests me.

53

George H. Doran,
25, West 32nd Street,
New York.
23rd November, 1911.

. . . In a fortnight I shall be (I hope) in your arms, and between your breasts. I shall see you and I shall know if you have changed, I mean physically. Otherwise you are not changed, I know it by your letters. The endings of your letters charm me and excite me, horribly. At the bottom of my mind is that every day here bores me, even though I am always amused or interested. Before I saw you I didn't have a moment's real peace. However, by the most extraordinary effort of willpower that I have ever accomplished, I have kept absolutely intact all my vital forces for you. It's killing me. My little one, one understands oneself, I imagine. You will never know exactly how and how much I love you; nobody knows it except me. But you almost know. I kiss you enormously.

Thy A.

Telegram

Bennett,   Liverpool.
26 Avenue des Champs Elysées.   5th December, 1911.
On disembarking after a fine voyage I kiss you.

Arnold.

CHAPTER VI

The Country House
and the Yacht

'The financial side of the affair,' he wrote to Mrs. Belloc Lowndes, referring to the trip to the States, 'is (for a modest realist) *fantastique.*' The proceeds indeed were such that he was able to rent, and later buy, a substantial house in Essex, and, furthermore, to give himself the luxury of a yacht. France had served its purpose, he was now a literary figure of firm and increasing fame and substance and he could return to England as *someone.* But he shrewdly chose to live in the country, as Mrs. Belloc Lowndes points out, to avoid the jealousies of the London literary world.

Shortly before leaving for the States he had already made up his mind to return to England.

Mme. A. Bennett,   Authors' Club,
Hotel Londres et New York,   London.
Paris.   15th September, 1911.
. . . Everyone is enchanted with the idea that we are going to live in England. Yesterday Marriott told me that his wife loves you more than no matter who, and that you were the only woman he knew of whom all the world said nothing but good. Never has he heard a word uttered against you. And so on, and so on.

  I embrace you and I kiss you and I leave you.
       Thy A.

MY ASSOCIATION WITH ARNOLD BENNETT *by Frederick Marriott*

I remember his making several fruitless excursions in company with his friend Atkins[1] in search of a house which would supply the modern equipment and standard of comfort he required.

---

[1] This was J.B. ('Johnny') Atkins, one-time editor of *The Spectator.*

They viewed many houses, but for one reason or another, none of them fully answered his purpose.

In addition to the luxurious yacht, he had bought a Lanchester car, which was then the best car on the market; so it was an easy matter for him to pursue his quest.

He liked an old house at Thorpe-le-Soken which had been built by French Huguenot refugees, but as it was devoid of modern conveniences he didn't think seriously about it.

However, when he took his wife round the district to look at some other houses which were advertised for sale (none of which found favour) she asked him to take her to see the old Huguenot house he had spoken of. When she saw it, she immediately fell in love with it, and saw the possibilities of both the house and its extensive grounds. Probably the Huguenot associations with the place had some influence on her enthusiastic appreciation of it.

Then followed consultations with Rickards, the architect, who went down with Arnold and inspected the property with a view to estimating the probable cost of alterations and additions; new bathrooms, decorations, lighting, etc., and eventually a letting contract was signed for four years, with the option of purchase at a fixed price, at the end of that time.

The house had the attractive name of 'Comarques', which, added to Thorpe-la-Soken, made a distinctive address.

It had been built early in Queen Anne's reign, a house of many windows, ivy-clad, with about three acres of lawn, lake, and garden attached. Colchester was some fourteen miles away, the small seaside resort of Frinton four, and his friend Atkins at Brightlingsea about seven, as the crow flies.

Rickards, by profession an architect, had central heating and three bathrooms installed. Arnold was given a bedroom and study, Marguérite her own bedroom and a boudoir, and after his secretary, Miss Nerney, had been allowed a room, only two rooms were left spare for guests until Marguérite had the idea of getting a local architect to create two more out of the attics.

Meanwhile he had taken a temporary lodging near his sister, Tertia, in Putney.

Mme. Arnold Bennett,　　　　　　14 St. Simons Avenue,
Hotel des Capucines,　　　　　　　　　　　　　Putney.
Paris.　　　　　　　　Tuesday, 22nd October, 1912.

Nouchette Chèrie,

Your letter. Very well. So, I wait for you to come on Saturday. Take the train that—well, take what train you wish. But get here in time for dinner. The Sharpes[2] will be at the theatre that evening. Mme. Sharpe said : 'But wouldn't Marguérite like to come with us?' 'Do you think so?' I asked myself, aside. I know that you wouldn't at all like to go out again that evening. That being so, I shall see all the things you have bought before the others, as also the person and the body that attracts (so it would seem) the attention of everybody in all the restaurants in Paris. This lingerie, this undress, this underwear, and all those little trinkets you are given for your dress, as much as the loved flesh they are fated to conceal. It's astonishing how much I miss you, after a week, and how your absence excites me every moment of the day. You can say that you have established an empire over me which, given my character etc., isn't an ordinary one. Take care not to abuse it, I beg you. It's the memory of you which excites me. During your absence I ought to have a little cocotte to comfort me. I suppose that you will come back with the *nichons* more enormous than ever, and all the curves extremely plump and rounded . . . I am anxious to see you in our castle. I flatter myself that those interiors will be better than the apartment in this awful house, which is as dry, arid, ugly, and cold as an old maid. I shall enjoy myself a lot in that house; a lot. It's a good find. The new servant came yesterday. She looks all right, but she is ugly . . . As for the carpets, very good. Tomorrow I have a rendezvous with Rickards to go into the question of cost—of everything! It will be terrible. I lunch with Lowndes.[3] I work well, and I feel marvellously well.

I shall inflict on you the last outrages. Don't defend yourself.

Thy A.　Nouche.

---

[2] Parents of Cedric Sharpe ,the 'cellist. Herbert Sharpe became a professor at the Royal College of Music.
[3] F. S. A. Lowndes, on the staff of *The Times,* husband of Mrs. Belloc Lowndes.

57

Mme. Arnold Bennett,   Putney.
Hotel des Capucines,
Paris.   24th October, 1912.

. . . If one single time more you write 'Comarques' with two
'M's' I shall chastise you and you will die of it. Mark what I
say !

Mme. Arnold Bennett,   The Reform Club,
Comarques,   London.
Thorpe-le-Soken,
Essex.   23rd February, 1913.

Infanta Cara,
    The first letter addressed to you in your palace is thus
addressed by your own husband, from his club, where he has
spent most of the day interviewing sundry gentlemen about his
business affairs. The said husband hopes that you aren't too
bored, vexed, and exasperated by the said palace.
                                          Thy A. Nouche.

While looking for a house in England he had meanwhile bought a
yacht. The latter indeed decided the location near the sea. He
might seem to have drifted into the world of yachts and yachting
by accident. When on his 'new honeymoon' at Cannes he had
gone down with a serious stomach upset that may have been
typhoid, and to convalesce he went to stay with John Atkins, at
Brightlingsea in Essex. Here he went sailing on Atkins's boat, the
Alan, and immediately the tone of his letters brightens : 'Today
I am feeling perfectly marvellous. We are just off for a sail. All
goes well. *La vie de yacht* is enchanting. It's the only thing.' So
of course nothing would satisfy him but to have a boat of his own,
and with money from the States he bought the *Velsa.*
    Even with a hired Duch skipper and a crew of two and her
auxiliary engine, she was an extraordinary boat for a beginner,
fifty-five feet long, flat-bottomed, and narrow enough to navigate

rivers and canals. Obviously not a boat for the North Sea! To him her great advantage was headroom and a large cabin in which he could work : 'I may say that I have never known another yacht that carried an encyclopaedia in more than a score of volumes.'

Yachts and yachting were a boyhood dream. As a boy he had built a model yacht so large that he hadn't been able to get it out of the attic he had built it in. Zest and a feeling of liberation fill his letters. Movement, new scenes, small emergencies, pride, salt air, were all suddenly necessary to him.

Mrs. Arnold Bennett,   Yacht *Velsa,*
Royal Albion Hotel,   Kingston, Surrey.
Brighton.   20th June, 1912.

Chérie adorée,

I have made the first voyage in the *Velsa.* We came from Ditton to Kingston (2 miles) where we are lying up for the night. I hope to have one of the crew here this evening from Brightlingsea. The boat goes admirably, and the captain is charming. Perhaps we shall get the third sailor (the cook) in London, while passing through, but it's not yet certain. We shall leave tomorrow morning at half-past six, and we shall arrive at Gravesend in the afternoon. Gravesend is at the end of the Thames estuary. Thence I shall come by car to you.

You were perfectly right with the hotel. Be firm and severe. I don't doubt that you are infinitely pleasing to my mother. If she charmed you as much, I should be pleased! ! ! ! Talking of the huge post yesterday, it's exactly this correspondence which is going to prove a bore. However, I shall tackle it all the same. While passing through London I hope to stop the boat opposite Pinker's [*whose address was in Arundel Street, which runs down to the Thames*] to pay him a business visit—give him the papers relating to the boat, etc. I have an awful story to tell about the bargaining with the ex-proprietor! But it's over and I will tell you all about it.

Until the outbreak of war in August, 1914, he made frequent trips in the *Velsa,* rarely with Marguérite. She, alas, was prone to seasickness. However, on the 30th August he was writing to her from La Haye (i.e. The Hague):

Today we begin varnishing the boat in honour of your arrival. I make myself perfectly understood by the crew—which is, apart from Willem—a bit stupid and dull, and it is to be desired that you don't tell me every time I chat with Edward that I make him tremble etc. etc. etc. etc. The weather is better, and the barometer is slowly climbing—a good sign.

To recapitulate. You will sleep on Monday night at the hotel at the Gare du Nord. On Tuesday morning you will take the 8.10 train for La Haye (the name of this town is 'La Haye' not 'Haye') where you will arrive at 4.37 in the afternoon. I shall be at the station. Ernest will be at the station to look after your luggage. We lie five minutes from the station. You won't have to change. There are two Customs stops—one in Belgium and one in Holland—but if you only have the valise they will inspect it in the train. That's all by way of directions. Come quickly. Be sure that I shall be alone. Rickards doesn't come until Sunday or Monday. The only thing I don't like here is your absence, and that troubles me enormously.

The following summer, however, when they had moved into the new house, he was writing a very different kind of letter to her:

Mme. Arnold Bennett,   Yacht *Velsa*,
Comarques,   Saturday morning.
Thorpe-le-Soken.   19th July, 1913.

Enfant chérie,
    It's now certain that I shall come back on Monday afternoon or evening. There are some certainties on this earth. Another certainty (I hope) is that the next time you want to rearrange my papers you will first express your intention to me and not to my clerquette (i.e. Miss Nerney, his secretary). Yesterday,

you felt that you had to tell me something about my clerquette. I also feel that I have to tell you something about my clerquette. It was impossible for her to conceal from me for twenty-four hours that my papers had been moved. But of course, since 'I see all' I noticed her first attempt to tell me while at the same time trying to be kind to you. 'What have you done with these papers?' I asked her. She blushed, and then she told me that madame wished to have the poster [*placard*]. Know, my child, that the dreadful disorder of my drawers that you deplore so much, is mine, and exclusively mine. (Ah, the lovely order in your own, my sweet child!) When I noticed that my clerquette didn't have a gift for organisation, I took it in hand myself, and I always take it in hand. No matter what business-man told you that whoever fills all his drawers is an idiot and a poor organiser. No matter what business-man told you that when papers of all kinds are coming in all the time one must have order. One can't earn 400,000 frs. per annum without having some poor papers. No matter what business-man told you that the organisation of my papers is marvellous. If you earned 400,000 frs. per annum with your pen, the entire house wouldn't be big enough to contain your papers. I would like to see you with your clerquette and your papers. I would very much like to see your cherished face if I played the game with Suzanne [Marguérite's maid] that you played with my clerquette (always with the best of intentions). Ah, the cries! The tears! The protestations! And if I had uttered the words 'bad faith' . . . it would have been the end of the world! . . . Là, là, là! What is unfortunate is that, in trying to be kind, my poor clerquette has done things with my papers that must be put right. Their present order is folly. In September I shall have to see to it. I shall have to get another piece of Empire furniture. It is always possible to attach too much importance to these personal matters. If all my papers were burnt I should get over it, I suppose. However, things without immediate importance sometimes have a moral importance that acute women always end by understanding. If you are acute, prudent, sensible, you will give me back the poster you filched from me, and you will give it back without saying anything. And you will wisely recollect that when you try to do things behind

my back, above all those things which closely concern me, you
will never succeed. We shall see. There was never any question
but that your intentions were perfect.

Love to the Mater. I embrace you tenderly,

> The cunning, artful husband who is not a
> friend, the man of bad faith. A.

P.S. You said : 'It's disgusting how he takes things so seriously.'
Not at all. I know you were joking. It's your privilege. I, too,
joke. It's my privilege.

Arnold Bennett Esq.,   Comarques,
Yacht *Velsa*.   Thorpe-le-Soken.
                                                 20th July, 1913.

Arnold chérie,

You shall have your poster. I was wrong to ask for it without
consulting you. But, acknowledge that your perpetual phrase,
when I ask for advice, 'Do what you like,' means nothing. Don't
say it ever again. *Give me orders.*

If I sometimes try to do what I like (that is, what I think best)
you undo everything I have arranged. Example . . . the blue
dovecot, the arrangements for getting the car to France. I am
enormously at fault because I am impulsive and because you
have authorised me to do what I like, but you must admit, my
dear, that you are at times capricious to say 'no' when somebody
tells you 'yes', and vice versa. These caprices I ought not to
criticise but, my dear, try changing nature !

Acknowledge that, for my part, when you ask the least thing
of me, I don't begin by saying 'no'.

There's something else I find a little unjust . . . If I earned
400,000 frs. with my pen, you say, the house would be full of
my papers. I have some papers of which I haven't the least idea
where they have got to, but then I haven't got a secretary to
arrange them for me . . . Also my work doesn't depend on papers
and pen. I don't pretend to be expert with them like that : but
I have, over six years, as evidence of my sense of organisation
and savoir-faire, furnished you with a house worthy of you by
reason of its order. Have you ever found anywhere in the house
dirty linen, clothes that needed mending, stains, dirty dishes—

and the thousand and one things that would offend you if I lacked the sense of organisation your imagination has taken from me? It's true I don't know how to earn a penny, but I pride myself on having got through life with a material and moral sense of order which has always guided me in even my most impulsive moments.

You did right to send me a letter telling me what was in your heart. I would always like you to do so when you are angry with me. Arguments between us become too serious. They upset you and bring an expression to your face which goes far to destroy my true feelings towards you and lessens the deep love and esteem I have for you. You take on this expression when I talk about some small thing and my southern temperament comes into conflict with your English temperament.

One thing is dear to me: it is that you remain happy. I am being only fair to myself when I say that I try to make you happy, and I suffer when the opposite happens. Good intentions are not enough . . . it's true . . . I have learned it only too well during the six years I have been your wife.

When you are tired of me you must say so. When one makes 400,000 frs. a year one hasn't the right to be unhappy—with that you can send me to the ends of the earth, for a time, if that is what you want.

Like you, I joke—only see in this my love.
I love you,
Marguérite.

A little more than six years after the wedding, this is the first storm of which the correspondence gives us a full record, hints though there are of previous such storms. However violent, however characteristic, however certain the warning of storms to come, he could still, a month later, cut short a wet holiday round the Danish coast to go back to her:

Mme. Arnold Bennett,   Yacht *Velsa*,
Comarques,   Aarhus.
Thorpe-le-Soken.   Monday, 24th August, 1913.
Chérie Enfant,
When I received your sweet letter this morning I decided to

make a big effort to catch the steamer on Wednesday, that is to say, the day after tomorrow, because there won't be another till Saturday but when I read that you had got it into your head that I was coming back tomorrow, Tuesday, I told myself : 'I'm off, and so much the worse for the exquisite water-colours that I was going to do!' *Only since Sunday* have we had fine weather. I perfectly understand the reasoning behind your letter. And in fact I was joking, so to speak. I am pleased that you have spread so much happiness, but I hope that you have saved a little for yourself.

The steamer from Esbjerg is supposed to get into Harwich at three o'clock on Thursday afternoon. Coming by car, it's the farthest of all the steamers—at the far end of the quay (which is very long). I wrote 4 o'clock in my wire because I don't think I shall be ready for the car before 4 o'clock. We shall leave Esbjerg at 4.45 Wednesday evening. I am happy all the same to be coming back sooner. It will give me two days in which to loaf with you before plunging back into my sacred work. As for the water-colours, I am definitely disgusted. Because of the bad weather I have scarcely done any, and now it's fine, I don't want to. That's funny.

I kiss you and I shall kiss you tenderly,
A. Nouche.

Marguérite aged 25

Arnold Bennett from a sketch by Frederick Marriott at
Les Sablons, August 1907

CHAPTER VII

The Operation

The staff needed to run Comarques consisted of a housekeeper (Stannard is the name one most often comes across), a parlour-maid, a second maid, and a cook. Miss Nerney was Arnold's constant secretary, and Fred Harvey his valet. The head gardener, Lockyer, had two under-gardeners working for him. Marguérite wrote in her Journal : 'Far too often she (Miss Nerney) is asked to give orders to the servants when it is my job to do so. And yet I can see why that happens. Am I not a foreigner who is incapable of making herself understood?' Yet the fact is that, in spite of a certain imperiousness, she inspired in the domestics a quite astonishing devotion. Lockyer was another matter, not surprising when this daughter of the Midi introduced hens, ducks, goats, rabbits, and swans, apart from Raton the Peke and John the fox-terrier. However, with the ducks she fell foul of Arnold who was so disturbed by their quacking that he gave orders for them to be sold; sold they were, but Marguérite replaced them with drakes, which are practically mute.

From Arnold's Journals[1] some idea can be gathered of how busy he was during the winter months with articles, novels, and plays. In February, 1914, for example, *Helen With the High Hand* had its première at the Vaudeville Theatre, London, and he had meanwhile been writing *The Price of Love,* for serialisation in *Harper's Magazine,* and *The Regent,* which had been published in September, 1913. Comarques, therefore, was fully serving its purpose as a quiet place in which to work and which afforded easy access on the one hand to the *Velsa* and on the other to London.

In March, 1913, Marguérite had suffered a serious, if short illness with a doctor and two nurses in attendance. Arnold commiserated with her on 'ton joli corps meurtri' in a letter written a year later while she was taking a cure at Vichy. But then, in July, 1914, an operation (for haemorrhoids) became necessary.

---

[1] Edited by Newman Flower and published in three volumes by Cassell & Co. Ltd. in 1932, and revised in Penguin Books, 1971.

I did not get better and arrangements were made for me to return to France to be operated on. Arnold took me to Thorpe station—and I arrived in Paris, alone, late in the evening. The nursing-home was situated at Neuilly, near Paris. I took a taxi and arrived there about midnight.

The nurse, realising who I was, asked, 'Where is your husband?'

'In England. I came over alone.'

'Fancy you coming here alone! Where is your maid?'

'I am alone,' I repeated.

She could not get over the fact that a patient, having to undergo an operation in two days' time, had travelled alone from England to Neuilly-sur-Seine.

Arnold Bennett Esq.,   c/o Dr. Bouteron,
Comarques,   Neuilly.
Thorpe-le-Soken.   July, 1914, before the operation.
. . . I hope to see you again, Arnold, my dear, but one never knows . . . here is what I would like you to do—after my death.

(1) During my mother's life send her 75 frs. a month and 360 frs. a year for her rent.

(2) Give Gabrielle (*her sister*) 50 frs. a month, and perhaps 600 frs. a year during her lifetime—the little that I can leave her would bring her in very little income. I would like what I have begun to be continued.

(3) My diamond should be given to Mary (Kennerley) and my travelling-bag to Tertia (Mary's mother).

Thy Marguérite.

Mme. Arnold Bennett,   Comarques,
c/o Dr. Bouteron,   Thorpe-le-Soken.
Neuilly.   Friday, 3rd July, 1914.
Chérissime,

We followed you all day yesterday, and at nine o'clock we said to each other : she's arrived. I hope it was true . . . I shall go to the yacht this afternoon and stay until Sunday evening.

Sullivan[2] will very probably go with me in his. He came yesterday to tea, but we didn't play tennis. I frantically hope that you won't let yourself be affected by this little operation which is to take place. Tell the doctor to wire me the result and everything immediately afterwards.

Mme. Arnold Bennett,   Yacht *Velsa*.
c/o Dr. Bouteron,
Neuilly.   Saturday, 4th July, 1914.
Ma petite chérie,
 I hope that your little operation is now over, and that you weren't too much upset by it. We are now (at half-past three) in the East Swale river, south of the Thames.

Mme. Arnold Bennett,   Yacht *Velsa*.
c/o Dr. Bouteron,
Neuilly.   Sunday, 5th July, 1914.
Ma très affectionnée,
 I was lying on my couch this morning in the port of Sheerness (in the Thames estuary) when Tadema [*one of the Dutch crew*] came into the cabin with a telegram thus worded : 'Operation over. Health satisfactory. Greetings, Bouteron.' So I hope all is well. I was very pleased to have the telegram. We left Sheerness immediately afterwards, and are now off Clacton.

Mme. Arnold Bennett,   Comarques,
c/o Dr. Bouteron,   Thorpe-le-Soken.
Neuilly.   Monday, 6th July, 1914.

Ma chère miniscule operée,
 . . . I can't work this morning. All this talk of operations upsets me. Perhaps I shall turn to this afternoon, but I don't know. On the boat I collected together my ideas and all that went well enough. Doubtless you will soon be given permission to write to your husband. I see you with your Mathilde (*a*

2 This was a neighbour, Herbert Sullivan, who was a nephew of the composer, Sir Arthur Sullivan.

French maid?) and your black hair on the pillow, and flowers all round you—everything except Raton.

And now I chastely embrace you, and that's all for the moment.

Nouche.

Mme. Arnold Bennett, Comarques,
c/o Dr. Bouteron, Thorpe-le-Soken.
Neuilly. 16th July, 1914.

Chèrie enfant,

Nothing from you yesterday. A nuisance. Two letters by today's midday post. Fine. It appears that you are better, and even much better. I don't know what to advise, but it seems to me that you would do much better to stay there awhile. While waiting you could go out once or twice. What I greatly fear is that on getting back here you will suddenly fall ill again, which would be very worrying for you, and for me, too.

No, I shan't come to fetch you. The pleasure of seeing you in Paris would be more than wasted by the irritations of the journey. You find me a bad traveller. I in turn find you a bad traveller. What good would it do? Just the satisfaction of seeing you 24 hours earlier? No, if you needed me, if it would help in any way, I would come at once, and you well know it. You will be much better with Jean [*perhaps her uncle, Jean Soulié, perhaps Dr. Bouteron himself*] than with me because you will be free to do whatever you want. I would a thousand times sooner see you here than anywhere else. I am *seriously* upset with my work. I don't think you can imagine just how much I am upset. But my health's all right, and the young girls [*visitors*] are sweet. However, to live with young girls doesn't mean anything to me.

Mme. A. Bennett, Yacht *Velsa*.
Comarques,
Thorpe-le-Soken. Friday morning, 31st July, 1914.

Mon enfant chérie,

The weather's fine. Although far from being cured, my liver

is much better. I also hope that you have got over trying to pass yourself off as a poor martyrised wife. It doesn't suit you. What I swallow with difficulty is you telling me that I do things behind your back, and make you out to be a madwoman. That's pure cheek, and you know it. You want a greenhouse. All right. Consultation between you, me, Canham, and Lockyer [*both gardeners*], and it's all fixed. Price, £15.17.0 or 400 frs. It's the most perfect of greenhouses and everybody is happy. But one fine morning the idea comes into your head of wanting two greenhouses. You order another on the spot. You give a firm order without having the least idea of the price. You know I am always in the house, but all this happens without my knowledge. It was purely by chance that I heard about it. You say that you forgot to tell me. No matter who told me. But it's a bit hard when you suddenly tell me that I do things behind your back. Untrue, totally. You say that you are surprised when I become obstinate. Untrue, totally. Together, the two greenhouses would certainly cost 1,000 frs. since the second is nearly twice the size of the other, which costs only 400 frs. I have no intention of making such an expenditure this year. It's obvious that the little house will be enough for what we get out of it this season. As for the following year, we shall see. Nobody yet knows if the greenhouse will be all right. All that we have yet to find out. When Warrington told me that you had ordered the second I said nothing. I started with you. I gave you my ideas on the subject, and then afterwards I told Warrington : 'Madame has made up her mind'. You will never be made to look like a madwoman because of me. The least that I ask is that I am consulted before definite orders are given about things which cost more money. You are mistress in the house, but I am master. I am the one who earns and pays out, and who directs the overall finances and it will always be me. Nineteen times out of twenty when you consult me I say yes . . . I myself am convinced that I am *very sweet* with you, as sweet as you are with me, and I shall die in this opinion. I am not an angel, but I don't know any angels. Ten times during the afternoon you interrupted what I was saying : you won't let me finish, and often you don't do me the honour of listening to me. I don't complain. But I am writing to you since I am at a distance. I know that you will read what I write. As a novelist, I don't ask more than that.

Putting aside this little session in the vast and magnificent sea of married life, I have to tell you that we are now in the Channel.

My child, I respectfully and affectionately salute you.

Thy Nouche.

MY ARNOLD BENNETT *by Marguérite*

A few days after I arrived back at Comarques, Arnold broke the news to me that he had arranged to go to Dieppe on his yacht and to cruise along the French coast, via Biarritz, with a friend.

The news surprised me in a way, yet I understood that he wanted a change. Yachting was the best relaxation for him. He had benefited to such an extent on the previous occasion that it would have been selfish of me to make any remark about his going away so soon after I had come back.

It was decided that he would leave Comarques at the very end of July and sail to Dieppe. I anxiously awaited to hear of his safe arrival, for the sea was rough. A few days later I had a wire from him, 'Just arrived Dieppe. War declared with Germany. Coming back. ARNOLD.'

Their differences of the previous month had not been improved by the interval.

Marguérite   Comarques,
(by hand)   Thorpe-le-Soken.
                                        Saturday, 22nd August, 1914.

Ma chère Marguérite,

The other day you came down into the little drawing-room expressly to tell me that if you had had the money you would long ago have left me, that you hated this life of snobbery and luxury, and that you would be much happier on your own with 500 francs a month.

Husbands who keep their wives solely by the hold they have over them in material things are idiots and worse. I consider that it is the duty of a husband to facilitate the departure of a wife who seriously wants to leave him. *If the other day you were serious,* I will guarantee you a maintenance—not of 500 frs.

but of 1,000 frs. a month. Take if you like your furniture which has cost more than 10,000 frs. and I will give you another 5,000 frs. towards the cost of installing yourself elsewhere. I am sure that I could furnish satisfactory guarantees. Anyway, I imagine that my word is good enough.

I write without ill-will and without bitterness and simply as a duty. It's true that I have already told you by word of mouth what I now state, but I would sooner put it into writing.

Thy A.B.

p.s. I forgot to tell you that as well I will make myself responsible for the rents that you are now paying for Gabrielle and your mother.

Marguérite.   Comarques.
(by hand)   23rd August, 1914.
Mon enfant,

Quarrels between you and me will never happen if I am left at peace in my sleep, my work, and the organisation of the garden, which I direct. Your misfortune and mine is that with the best of intentions you forget. A quarrel has already occurred about the maids, whom you have instructed to get up at 5.30. I complained; I explained to you at length that I couldn't do with it, and you changed it at once. But it appears to have started again. I again complained, but this time you were more obdurate. You told me that if I could neither sleep nor work, so much the worse—that it was absolutely necessary for the maids to get up at 5.30. So that the maids shan't be inconvenienced and the house managed according to programme, you have even suggested that I leave this house which exists exclusively for me! Naturally in the end your commonsense prevailed. . . . It's absurd. It's absolutely as though my peace of mind, my work, my sleep, counted for nothing. I know that they count but nobody else ever says so. You tell me to do what I like. I give definite instructions. Immediately, without anyone having told me what's going on, my instructions are countermanded. Always with the best of intentions, but the result is that during the night I am once more upset. All this won't stand up as a general way of life. It cannot continue. When you are reorganising the house, make up your mind if you want the services of a man or not. If the answer is yes, I will give you a man, and I will organise the garden separately. The two things can't be run together when every time the house runs short it robs the garden. The house ought to be self-sufficient. I won't say for the moment, but later on when you are reorganising, don't count on a gardener to polish the shoes or clean the knives, and on a chauffeur to clean out the stove, etc. etc. *I repeat—I don't say for the moment.* But don't wait for the war to end before doing your reorganising. The war could last a year. It will never be an economy in this place to cut down on servants or to upset me in things which mean so much to me. Each upset costs ten times more than you can save in a year, or more. This week we have lost at least 4,000 frs. I return your affection.

Thy A.B.

Nouche.

P.S. I think that's enough letters, now.

THE MERRY WIVES OF WESTMINSTER *by Mrs. Belloc-Lowndes*

He [Arnold] had no knowledge of how an English country house ought to be run, and he compelled his wife to manage Comarques exactly as his mother had managed her small house in the Five Towns. The household stores were dealt out each day with parsimonious care, and anything in the way of special food was locked up after each meal; yet Bennett would spend in one week, when staying in a London hotel, far more money than he would permit his wife to spend at Comarques in a month.

Marguérite's Journal

At times I did not dare pick the flowers in the garden, and I had the impression that the servants thought I was mad—for my orders were barely understood, or if they were, they were often altered by my husband. My dearest husband could not see my point when I would explain to him the ridiculous position he put me in. As ever, he wanted to bend me to his way of thinking and doing. His great principle is that a husband should never give way to his wife whether she be right or wrong. He says that one of the married pair has the right to be 'in command'; that one, of course, is the husband. Arnold is a leader, and he wants me to understand clearly that I am to follow and obey. I have to accept his views on the running of the house. Here are the most important of the unwritten laws:

(1) the Garden is my own (i.e. Arnold's) department. It is forbidden to interfere with it in any way.

(2) Wife and servants are another department, but he will give them any order he likes.

(3) The house is his and he will furnish it how he pleases. Once he says a piece of furniture goes in a certain place, it stays there forever.

(4) He organises his life as he chooses. He has time only for writing. As for me, his wife, I must be happy, smile, and always be on time. I must look after myself. Also see that the meals are good and the house is well attended to. My duty is to see that he is not disturbed when he is trying to sleep as he is a very bad sleeper.

(5) He is the one who knows about business. I can rely on him because what he understands he always manages well. When the time comes, if ever, when he must talk to me about his money affairs, he will do so. Meanwhile if I ever ask him questions about finance he will reply that it is a very complicated business which would take days to explain, in fact weeks and years before I would be able to understand even a bit—and even then he doubts if I would understand.

(6) He gives me so much money a week for the housekeeping and so much a year for my clothes. If by any chance anyone in our family needs help, he will help, as it is his duty as a husband to do so.

Doubtless the outbreak of war, a little over seven years after their wedding in Paris, and its continuance, helped the decline in their relationship. He became intensely preoccupied with journalism. Staff began to be called up, or to leave. The *Velsa* was taken out of commission and brought inland with other yachts so that they could not be used by an invading enemy. Wounded began to arrive at the local hospital. Arnold accepted the unlikely post of Military Representative on the local Emergency Committee for preparation against invasion.

As for Marguérite, she helped with a Soldiers' Club in London, and is now and then discovered journeying up to town with Arnold, but only to lunch with Rickards or go to a concert. Their one joint excursion was to attend the funeral of his mother, 'the Mater', in November, at Burslem. Chiefly she was idle, her job principally to see to the smooth-running of the house and to act as hostess to the guests whom Arnold invited, although she had found another outlet in entertaining troops who were billeted locally.

MY ASSOCIATION WITH ARNOLD BENNETT *by Frederick Marriott*

When I paid one of my surprise visits to Comarques in the early days of the Great War, I found that troops were stationed at Thorpe-le-Soken taking part in the defences of the East coast, and the village had become very active.

Arnold Bennett and his wife were doing everything they could for the benefit of the troops. They had a large wooden hut constructed in their grounds, and equipped it with a stage and piano, tables, chairs, and a good variety of games, such as chess, draughts, cards, etc. It constituted a kind of club-house which was available for the recreation of the soldiers whenever they pleased.

There was a plentiful supply of tea, coffee, and soft drinks served by Mrs. Bennett and willing helpers from the village whom she had enlisted to assist with the work.

Entertainments were organised which discovered performers among the officers and men of the army, and which were augmented by local talent. These entertainments provided a rich fund of pleasure for all concerned, and were much appreciated. Arnold Bennett was so busily engaged in London on official work, that he couldn't actively co-operate in these jolly affairs, which were entirely arranged by his wife. I well remember the pride with which she told me that she had sung an old French popular song at one of his concerts, and that 'the Tommies loved it'. With a characteristic ripple of laughter she said : 'And now I am the favourite artiste of the company.'

In the spring of the following year (1915) a prolonged and bitter correspondence began to be exchanged between the two on the subject of the gardener, Lockyer. Marguérite disliked him, and Arnold supported him because he was a capable workman in days when labour was rapidly becoming scarce. To quote all the letters in full adds nothing to our knowledge of the two or of the marriage, but it is necessary to note that Arnold, who was rapidly becoming one of the country's foremost voices of opinion, and who had only recently begun to write his latest novel, *A Lion's Share*, could still find time to place a five-page letter on his wife's dressing-table containing the following :

Marguérite.   Comarques.
(by hand)   10th April, 1915.

Enfant,

    . . . I take this opportunity to tell you something that is close to my heart—that you have plenty of talent and as much charm, but the price you exact is too dear, and I cannot go on paying it. There are too many, and much too many, grievances, quarrels, and scenes humiliating both to you and me, both here and in London. I cannot go on living in this bizarre world in which all the servants are fools, all the gardeners knaves, the secretary stupid, the chauffeur a fellow who does nothing, and the mistress of the house a martyr. You complain too much, you are too often discontented, you criticise too much, and you create too many rows. It's true that you suffer from neuralgia. But you aren't the only one who suffers such ills. Like you, I have hereditary weaknesses. I am also aware that you have a different temperament which tends to make you melancholy. But there are limits beyond which you ought not to go. You really have no right to behave towards me as you do behave— doubtless unconsciously. The scenes in which you involve me

76

are unheard-of—and for nothing. Come what may, you must have a grievance, if not a big grievance, a small one; but you must have one. I remember, and I shall remember all my life, the scene you created in front of Pinker, because I would not give you enough money! Such a scene was inexcusable and unforgettable. Now it's the car. If I made a martyr of myself as you do, what would you say? A change is absolutely necessary because my life is becoming poisoned, and all your charm and all your talent won't be enough to prevent a catastrophe. You grumble, you criticise, you make accusations, you make a martyr of yourself—and I don't know if you yourself see it! But I seriously beg you to think about it. If you find that, as always, you are perfectly in the right and that I am perfectly in the worng, in the end you will force me to leave you. I am not a Sharpe [*this was Herbert Sharpe*] and I am not exclusively a machine for making money. And I advise you to consider me a little, because I am on the way to becoming dangerous.

Thy A.B.

Marguérite's reply was left in turn on *his* dressing-table.

Arnold.   Comarques.
(by hand)   Tuesday, 13th April, 1915

Mon cher Arnold,

You are always irritated when once in three months I complain or talk about your gardener. I profoundly detest this man who has just as much detestation of me. Since you talk about leaving me, now is your chance. Either Lockyer goes, or I do. This time I shan't change my mind. So choose.

The fact that for two years I have put up with a servant who dislikes me and who has no respect for me, because you uphold him, should surely be enough reason for you to get rid of him. I don't know when I was last alone with you to have the opportunity or the wish to tell you my little worries. You don't understand them. You will never understand them. By nature I am open. It is necessary for me to tell you what I think about other people as well as about myself. At table, when people are about, is my only chance. Because you don't allow me to tell you my worries openly when we are alone, I have to do so in front of others. This morning anything I said would have made you angry unless it was in praise of the gardener.

Only one thing will be changed if I leave; the absence of someone of another nation in this place, Comarques, who is your exclusive property. Your English domestics I don't understand.

Allow me to return into obscurity. If I shan't be happy there at least I shan't weary you with the complaints you find so excessive. You know better than I do your duty towards me . . . Tell me what you decide and I will leave before Thursday when I am to engage more maids, a task I abandon with pleasure.

I haven't the right to make you unhappy, but no more have you the right to forget that I ought to have your sympathy.

Decide about Lockyer, and I will have my luggage packed.

I embrace you and leave you without bitterness.

Your wife,
Marguérite.

Marguérite   Comarques.
(by hand).   13th April, 1915.

Ma chère Marguérite,

It isn't a question of choosing between you and Lockyer. It's a question of deciding who—you or I—is going to take the initiative in things which are my concern and for which I am responsible.

I don't know if you have given the challenge you have presented me enough thought. I don't think so. It is a serious challenge. And if you go on with it, I will give it to you. If I told you: 'Choose—either I will manage the house according to my own ideas, and show the servants the door as I like, or I will leave you,' you would be the first, independent as you are, to tell me: 'All right, leave me!'

Thy A.B.

I was firmly resolved to leave Comarques for good if he did not give way to me on such an issue. I kept on saying to myself : 'But what a tragedy to be caused by a gardener!' But I was sure that I was right in asking such a sacrifice of my husband. Arnold's answer was not long in coming. I found it on my writing-table an hour later. It all went to say that, 'I will not give notice to the gardener, and nothing will induce me to change my mind.'

I tried to keep calm, and I replied : 'As you have decided, I shall catch the morning train. Please ask our guests to excuse me and give them whatever explanations you like.' I put the letter in Arnold's study. I rang the bell for the maid to prepare my bed for the night and to bring in my trunk etc., and told her that I did not want to be disturbed.

I shivered and my head ached. I closed my eyes and tried to collect my thoughts. My husband wanted to have the upper hand because he believed that our happiness would be greater if he was the unquestioned master. Misunderstandings had to end and I had to go—yes, he would certainly be happier without me. I thought my heart would burst—I cried and cried and cried—I sobbed my heart out. Was I not to lose everything in the next few hours? I had about £2 loose in cash and £30 in the bank. When that was finished, what would happen?

At about 8 o'clock I could hear voices and a burst of laughter coming from the drawing-room beneath my room. Oh, heavens! To be laughing while such a tragedy was taking place over their heads! I sobbed my heart out—I could not keep back the flood of tears.

My bedroom door opened and I heard someone shut it again. It was Arnold. He found me on my couch still sobbing. He asked me what was the matter and I was unable to answer. He also was very miserable and his voice faltered. I cannot remember how long this lasted, but I remember that he helped me into bed, and that he sat on the edge of the bed and asked again : 'What is the matter?'

'I am miserable because I have got to leave you.'

'Why,' he said. 'That is not necessary.'

'Yes, because you do not want to do what I ask.'

He answered angrily : 'About giving notice to the gardener?
Never. He is staying.'

I remember I made some excuse for having upset him, the
very thing I should not have said, and he left me, well aware
that in doing so he forced me to leave Comarques. I also realised
this and suddenly I did not suffer so intensely. I realised that
something in me no longer existed, and that I had lost my love
for my husband.

I fell asleep, and in all probability my husband was sleeping
the sleep of the just as well. I woke about midnight and my
head was still aching but I said to myself, No, I shall not go.
Some mysterious power was making me realise that I was a fool
to finish with my home just because I refused to tolerate a
gardener and a husband who is too difficult to understand.

The Lockyer dispute was far from decided. Bitter letters about
him were still to pass between them until Lockyer was called up.
When he returned in 1918 the quarrel about him again broke
out but he finally solved the problem by leaving of his own accord
for another job.

That summer, in the interests of journalism, Arnold was invited
to visit France and the front line.

Mme. Arnold Bennett,   Hotel Meurice,
Comarques,   Paris.
Thorpe-le-Soken.   Monday evening, 28th June, 1915.

Enfant chèrie,

At last I am back in Paris. Thanks for your two telegrams.
I am tired out. Otherwise I am all right. I couldn't put up with
more than three consecutive days of such sensation. We were
treated like princes. We saw everything. Yesterday morning
we went into the front line trenches at Bethune. The men were
superb. The relationship between officers and men is most
admirable. We were within 400 metres of the Germans. The
commanding officer offered us some champagne. An amazing

Marguérite from a sketch by Frederick Marriott at Les Sablons,
August 1907

Marguérite 1916. From the portrait by Edouard Ermitage

chap! At that very moment a German shell landed in the corner of the farmyard where his canteen was. While running for it we were much exposed. When we had jumped into a communication-trench another shell exploded within 60 ms. of us, and then a third. You could hear them coming. Everyone threw themselves to the ground until the explosion. We walked *4 or 5 ks*. through communication-trenches. We lunched very well at Rheims (Hotel du Nord). The cathedral had been bombarded the same morning. Nobody seemed to think much of it. Papers were being sold at the very spot where a shell had landed an hour before.

I am exhausted. I embrace you and I kiss you tenderly.

Nouche.

Mme. Arnold Bennett,   Hotel Meurice,
Comarques,   Paris.
Thorpe-le-Soken.   30th June, 1915.
Chère enfant,

I received your two letters of Monday yesterday, Wednesday. Before that I had only had one letter and two telegrams. I have written something to you everyday. You do well not to be aggrieved about the two tickets for Cedric's concert. [*i.e. that of Cedric Sharpe, the 'cellist*]. You insisted so often before the last concert that you didn't want to go, and that if you went it would be against all inclination, that I decided not to ask you to go to any more concerts, above all when I couldn't go with you. I haven't got a single ticket for the second concert. I simply gave Cedric two guineas and told him to give the tickets to whomsoever he liked—if he wanted to. I also told him what I think is true, that you would be busy at Thorpe with arranging jumble-sales etc. If I had asked you if you wanted to go to the concert you would most certainly have said that you didn't want to, and that it would bore you.

You remind me that I criticised you. I can tell you one thing, which is that you have criticised me *a thousand times* more bitterly than I have criticised you.

Don't think for a moment that your remarks have hurt me. Not the least little bit. I defend myself, that's all.

81

His thoughts on their way of life in wartime are contained in a letter from Glasgow, whither he had gone for a revival of *Milestones*, date 14th December, 1915.

When you think about it you will find that all kinds of things have changed in our everyday existence. No more yacht. A servant the less. No more chauffeur. A little car instead of a big one. Frank will soon be in the army. The loafer leaves us at the end of the year. [*Frank was one of the staff, the 'man' or handyman whom Marguérite had demanded for the house.*] As well, we have spent around 25,000 frs. less this year than in the twelve months preceding the outbreak of war. The last thing one ought to change in a household, above all in the household of an artist, still more of two artists, is normal routine. And we have arranged it on such a modest footing, relative to our income, that a change isn't necessary. Besides, when one has a house, one has a house. Either one keeps it or one leaves it. To leave it would cost us decidedly more dear than to keep it. The alternative is London, where our expenses would be doubled. I must have a room to work in, and another for Miss Nerney, and the house's value would be lost; it's always necessary to heat it and do necessary repairs. So we will remain in our niche, and go our way as before, if servants allow. As always you are free to spend your money as seems best to you. I only ask you that you won't be too upset when by some accident you can't have the car for a day or two. I fancy that, after the war, if nothing untoward happens, we will take a flat in *Londrinette* . . .

In spite of everything, the long nagging letters that would have proved fatal to any other marriage, the war, the essential lack of unity between the two, the marriage persisted.

Marguérite.   Comarques.
(by hand)   28th January, 1916.

Enfant chérie,
    Your letter, which I found by chance, was very sweet. I will

try to reply with the same sweetness. I recognise that from time to time it's difficult for you, and I'm sorry. But it doesn't often happen. Nineteen times out of twenty, on going to bed, you suddenly appear in my room to say goodnight, and disappear at once; a habit that is often a little irritating. Yesterday evening when you came into my room I thought it was to say goodnight. You know my ideas regarding the sacred rite of going to bed— an idea which is perhaps a trifle poetic and artistic, but one that is easy to satisfy. You said : 'Is it goodnight, or—?' and I said : 'It is goodnight.' You said : 'Well, I will come into your bed for three minutes.' I must remind you that on Monday you came back from London excited by pleasure while I was poorly and exhausted—after having worked all day for the soldiers, whom, it appears, the French love more than the English. I had no idea that you were annoyed. I was extremely surprised by your tears. It all cost me a bad night, the third in succession, and it was no fault of mine.

Having made that clear, I am at liberty and anxious to embrace you, and to assure you of my sincere love.

Thy Nouche.

CHAPTER IX

Wife to a Creative Artist

It became necessary for him to take rooms in 'Londrinette' sooner than he had foreseen because journalism was claiming more and more of his attention. In this year (1916) he finished *The Lion's Share* and wrote the play *Carlotta* for the actress Doris Keane, and every week, sometimes two or three times, he was coming to London. He visited his clubs, notably the Reform and the Royal Thames Yacht Club, and attended dinners, art shows, concerts, and above all committees not so much for their own sakes as to gather information and keep his thumb on the pulse of opinion.

In August he took a short holiday with Marguérite in Scotland, and in September a longer, sketching holiday at Corfe, in Dorset, with the artist John Wright. ('I shall not return to your arms till Monday,' he wrote. 'I am learning much. I kiss you *Arnoldement.*')

But then, in October, so as to be able to stay in London throughout the week, he rented a flat at the Yacht Club, a situation which he described as 'rather like celibate life in Paris again'. Marguérite was alarmed. She saw in this move a threat to her possession of him.

Mme. Arnold Bennett,	Royal Thames Yacht Club,
Comarques.	80 Piccadilly,
	London, W.1.
	26th October, 1916.

My dear Marguérite,

. . . I will not have any more scenes about my room here. I have already had too many, and one that I shall not immediately forget. I took a room here permanently because I can keep in it all sorts of things necessary to my work, and because it is cheap. I didn't take it for pleasure, but for business. It was necessary for me, and necessary *at once*. I can't postpone such decision for weeks. Every week lost is a week lost. My novel [*this was a new one, 'The Roll Call'*] has got to go on. I already have quite enough difficulty with my novel, without extraneous difficulties. You can call it a bedroom, or an office, or what you like, but I have got to have it. And you have no right whatever to be furious about it. You have always said you wanted a small cheap flat, without servants. Have it, by all means.

Eventually Marguérite found such a flat at Thackeray Mansions, 52 Oxford Street, London, W.1. They then found themselves running three establishments, because of course they kept using Comarques periodically, and married life with the Bennetts became even more a matter of letters, of appointments to see each other, and inevitably of marital rights, wrongs, and jealousies.

Mme. Arnold Bennett,   Royal Thames Yacht Club,
52 Oxford Street,   80 Piccadilly,
London, W.1.   London, W.1.
                25th January, 1917.

My lonely girl,
    I was sorry I was obliged to leave you all alone this after. You must learn to amuse yourself in London. You have friends —and friends who would be delighted to spend an evening with you when I am engaged, but you will always have to make such arrangements beforehand. You knew on Friday last that I should be otherwise engaged on Mon., Wed., and Thurs. evening of this week. So it was necessary for you to arrange things for yourself. If you leave it until the evening arrives you will always be disappointed because London doesn't live like that. Last week I spent three evenings out of four with you, but that can't always happen.
                I kiss you tenderly,
                Nouche.

Marguérite.   Comarques.
(by hand)   Friday, 26th January, 1917.

My dear child,
    ... I will dine with you on Wednesday evening. I had another

appointment (with Rickards) but I can change it. The fact is that I am always glad to be alone with you, and I don't grow bored. This morning I failed to send my work to the devil and come to see you. But I am too preoccupied to allow myself such whims.

Mme. Arnold Bennett,   Royal Thames Yacht Club,
52 Oxford Street,   80 Piccadilly,
London, W.1.   London, W.1.
                                            15th February, 1917.

My dear Marguérite,

... I cannot, save very exceptionally, lunch with you when I am in London. I do not come to London for pleasure. It is absolutely necessary for my articles and my work that I should see a great deal of businessmen, politicians, etc., and I can only see them at lunch-time. I work all the time; I have a great deal to do; I have a large number of anxieties of all sorts. All my lunches are for the purpose of my work, and they are very valuable to me. In fact they are essential. Evenings are quite different. I usually *do* dine with you, each week. I have spent three evenings with you *de suite*. I could have spent two evenings with you this week, but you are engaged. You asked me to dine with you tonight. But you did not ask yourself what I should do after dinner. Was I to go back and work, or was I to go to bed? You surely did not expect me to go and see that desolating play [*My Lady's Dress*] of Knoblock's again. You surely must realise the awful, bad effect of such plays on an artist. Or don't you?

I shall not come to see you this morning. I cannot do it. You are always saying: '*Je ne peux rien dire,*' etc., etc., but when anybody else says anything, even if it is only in reply to you, you get angry. You say it is irritating for you to control yourself. Of course it is. It is irritating for everybody to control himself. Nevertheless self-control is essential in any regular and organised society. ...

By the end of April he had finished *The Roll Call,* and a week later the idea came to him for another novel, which eventually became *The Pretty Lady*. Marguérite and he met by arrangement either at Comarques or at her flat, but she was to learn that the conjugal habit was not always acceptable to him.

Mme. Arnold Bennett,   Reform Club,
Comarques.   Pall Mall,
                                              London, S.W.
                                     Tuesday, 15th June, 1917.

Chérie enfant,

It is undeniable that I have been very much upset. Thanks to a drug that Mrs. Webb [*this was Mrs. Sydney Webb, later Lady Passfield*] gave me I am now a lot better. . . . I slept all right. For six hours. I feel that I am perpetually in the threatening shadow of work which must be done. I imagine that if you understood a bit better what the work of a creative artist is like you would not have told me that it is my duty—and that I knew it—to sleep away from here [*i.e. at Marguérite's flat*] on Wednesday and Thursday. The process of writing is so delicate, so easily thrown off-balance, that I have given up trying to explain it to you. But I can tell you that work begins immediately on waking, that it is an ever-present preoccupation, and that to wake up in a strange bed in strange surroundings, and to be forced to leave them and adopt new surroundings before beginning to write, is very frustrating, and might well spoil a whole morning's work. But it is useless trying to explain such things. One knows about them, or one doesn't know about them, that's all.

I hope to see Mr. Atkins ('*Johnny*') tomorrow.
                        I kiss you tenderly,
                                Nouche.

Arnold Bennett Esq.,   Comarques,
Reform Club,   Thorpe-le-Soken,
Pall Mall,
London, S.W.   20th June, 1917.

Mon chéri,

I am glad you are better. If you would explain yourself more often nothing but good would come of it. I don't deserve to be told that I don't understand the work of a creative artist (for your letter said as much). If I don't understand it, how could I have managed to remain these last ten years the wife of a creative artist? He would have told me to go to the devil a long time ago. I have always accepted what you are impelled to do. It's very natural that I don't always accept it in silence. I must be able to reserve some right over my creative artist husband. Certainly I understand that from the moment of waking you must be the slave of what you are writing! It can't be otherwise. One day I shall perhaps learn to organise my whole life and my feelings as though I didn't have a man for a husband but only a creative artist husband.

I kiss you, Nouche,

Thy Marguérite.

Marguérite's Journal

I am sorting out my personal papers—all my husband's letters to me since we were married. There are a good many of them. I read some of them and they are all characteristic of him. I cannot imagine that I am the woman to whom they are sent. In general he seems to treat me like a naughty child who has everything to learn. In turn I have always seen him as a difficult man who is in need of a friend who could square up to him and tell him frankly what he thought of him. Not one of his friends has ever done that. And not one has ever loved him enough to do so. Moral courage is the virtue of very few human beings.

Marguérite   Comarques.
(by hand).   4th July, 1917.

My dear Marguérite,

. . . Two years ago you shut the folding doors of the drawing-room in defiance of my wishes, and they remained shut ever since until the other day you suddenly discovered that the doors were much better open and you opened them. You completely altered the furniture of the small drawing-room, also, in defiance of my wishes. I am not complaining of these things, I am stating them.

. . . I agree to your giving a charity ball. I detest balls myself, but am quite willing to agree to it to please you, and you on your part say that the house shall be put straight immediately aferwards. What happens? *Without consulting me,* you entirely change the disposition of two rooms and the hall—the most important part of the house. Supposing that, *without consulting you,* I went and changed the look of the house—you would think I had gone mad and you would be extremely angry. If you ask me whether really I don't like the new arrangement, my answer is that I certainly do not. It is very bad and banal artistically, and it is impossible for the piano. There is only one safe place for the piano, and that is where it was. A piano is not a table; it is a very delicate instrument. I know that you did not know this, but you know now that I have told you. Unless both doors are kept closed the piano ought not to remain where it is still; it has already been there much too long, but I will agree to the piano risking its life a little longer. I am sorry that you should have to receive this letter on your wedding-day; but you should have chosen your dates differently.

Ton mari vieillard qui te bise,
Nouche.

The above is a shortened version of a much longer letter of protest and reproach, on the envelope of which, in English, in Marguérite's handwriting, are the words : 'After a ball, received from Arnold on our 10th wedding-day.'

Arnold   Comarques.
(by hand).   Summer, 1917.

My dear Arnold,

You hate leaving anything in my hands. Little by little every interest I had or have is taken from me. At times I feel absolutely unnecessary and wonder why I am in this house at all. I said nothing rude to you. I told you in French what I was thinking. I told you that it is always the same : I don't insult but tell the perfect truth. Of course, I am always in the wrong. Everybody knows that I shall always be so . . . But I give you my word that I shall no longer interest myself in things that concern the house; as for my husband, I shall interest myself in him only when he lets me.

. . . If you cannot accept me as I am, then say so. You will not really miss me as much as you believe. You don't really need my help except in keeping the house full of people. My flat in London will suit me very well. I will get a maid, and you can have this house to yourself, unorganised. You can manage everything yourself. Cook knows your ways; the parlour-maid knows them; and I should imagine that by now Miss Nerney knows them. Just tell me what you want.

Now that I have said what I must, I shall feel able to entertain our guests tonight. I always shall be furious when consciously or unconsciously you don't play fair with me. If you really feel that I was rude in front of the young people, then I apologise, but I still feel that I had every reason, dissatisfied as I am with my share of our married life.

That's all,
Your Marguérite.

Marguérite's Journal

Once my flat was in order I had hoped that Arnold would join me there, at least for the night, as I had two bedrooms, one of which was fixed up specially for him. However, he only came very occasionally, and then he would always sleep in my bedroom as the bed was larger, with the result that I had to sleep in the other room! In the end, I sent his bedroom furniture down to Comarques and used that room [*i.e. the room she had originally furnished as Arnold's bedroom*] as a dining-room. This arrangement allowed me to have a really nice sitting-room.

One cannot resist remarking that the arrangement also meant that, when Arnold spent the night at the flat, he would have to sleep in Marguérite's bed.

Arnold's influence as a journalist had become such that, in late October, 1917, he had been invited to Ireland by the G.O.C.,

Ireland, Intelligence Department. From Dublin he wrote as follows:

Mme. Arnold Bennett,   Dublin.
52, Oxford Street,
London, W.1.   Friday, 2nd November, 1917.
I have not checked this letter. A.

Mon enfant chérie,
     Yesterday I received with pleasure your letter of Wednesday evening, written alone in the flat. It's not pleasant that you find yourself alone, but one cannot have the pleasure of society without the drawbacks of society. Doubtless you perceive that the war is going to go on much longer. What I have to say is that I shall become more and more busy. You will acknowledge that I already spend the greater part of my evenings with you, in London. I shall not be able to do this any longer because my days (are becoming) quite another thing. In any case I shall be at the flat on Tuesday evening, if you want me to sleep there. I very much like sleeping there, on the sole condition that I have nothing much to do the following day. It is impossible for you to be blind to the fact that I am always happy when I am peacefully with you. I don't know whether I can bring my night-things with me just for Tuesday evening. I daresay I can manage, or you can manage it for me. I hope you have all your things in London. I have always felt sorry that you didn't buy that little black thingummy we saw in the shop near the Queen's Hall that afternoon we visited the Michaelis' flat. [*Lieut. Michaelis was an Australian R.E. officer who had stayed with the Bennetts at Comarques in the early days of the war.*] I notice that recently you lack some of these *nouveautés nocturnes*.
     Today I am exhausted. Yesterday I was in Belfast, and that finished me. I have a headache. Luckily I have no big thing on this after(noon). But this morning I was very busy. I leave tomorrow morning, Saturday, by the 6.40 boat. I shall sleep at the club until Tuesday.
                         I kiss you well,
                                   Nouche.

What sort of marriage was this, one wonders, in which the husband likes to visit his wife's flat and sleep with her only when he doesn't have much to do next day? For some mysterious reason, possibly Arnold's absolute belief in the rightness of what he is doing, the normal condition of marriage, in which husband and wife occupy the same house, if not the same bed, is made to appear exceptional. In such a case, when husband and wife daily exchanged letters, complained when they didn't precisely know where the other was and what he or she was doing, yet had few common interests and no real home, what fundamentally held them together? Why did they remain married? What was there in it for either of them?

Marguérite is the easier to understand. She was given all the money she needed; from hanging about the fringes of Parisian literary and stage circles she had become the wife of a celebrity in London with a wide circle of celebrities for acquaintances; she was given freedom to fulfil herself as hostess, canteen-worker, or reciter of advanced French poetry. Over and above these advantages, she loved him. There is absolutely no evidence to lead one to think otherwise. She swears that this was the case when she married him, her two books affirm it, her letters are filled with the authentic notes of admiration, pity, condolence, and heartbreak, and thirty years after his death she was still grieving for him.

A strong sense of duty, as we have seen, was impressed on Arnold. He had paid for his sister, Emilie's, divorce; he had saved another sister, Sissie, from the worst effects of her husband's bankruptcy; he supported his mother, he even supported Marguérite's mother and sister. Marguérite was his wife, therefore she above all must be respected, maintained, and saved from her follies.

As well as his duty to his wife, he still had, ten years after marrying her, an admiration for her orginality, her ability to outshine at, for example, Opening Day at the Royal Academy, and her style. Having a wife was still a social advantage, and having a French wife was still something to be proud of. He was dependent upon her sexually, for constitutionally, out of inbuilt reserve, it is extremely doubtful if he could have brought himself to undertake a chance liaison. (Once, yes, he did. For *The Pretty Lady* he drove himself personally to find out what sleeping with a pick-up was like, and for weeks afterwards was haunted by fears of clap. I shall not forget, when this story went round the family, either my mother's high, moral indignation, or my father's amusement, bearing in mind that the one was Arnold's sister and the other a fellow who had known Arnold as a youth.) Arnold seems to have been titillated by black lingerie and *nouveautés nocturnes*. Consistent with the man, his sexual habits could only have been transferred from Marguérite with the greatest difficulty and embarrassment.

Moreover, the effort needed to obtain a divorce, or even a separation, and the emotional disturbance that would go with either, was something he could not yet face, whatever Marguérite's vagaries: besides, divorce or separation would imply failure on his part, and any kind of failure was unthinkable.

Her rearrangement of the Thackeray Mansions flat did not pass unnoticed: 'I don't understand your new arrangement of the flat,' he wrote, 'and I wonder where you have pushed the other bed. In any case on Tuesday we shall be able to sleep together in the big bed, and I shall take a sleeping-draught to make me sleep. I haven't taken one for 15 days, and the doctor said I might take one once a week.'

This bed he was wondering about was of course part of the furniture Marguérite had sent down to Comarques. She may have thought she had outwitted him, but he could still escape her with the help of a sleeping-draught.

CHAPTER X   A Complication of Houses

In a letter dated 10th January, 1918, Arnold wrote a long letter
from Comarques to Marguérite at her Oxford Street flat repeating
his arguments for not coming to live with her. It went on as
follows :

. . . I cannot continue to be menaced every few days by this
idea of going to live in London. I simply will not do it, and
rather than do it I would live here alone.

Now about *your* work. I did not say anything about your
returning here on Saturday evenings instead of Friday evening,
because you had arranged it without consulting me. It was
therefore useless for me to say anything. However, I greatly
object to it. Then, within less than a week of telling me that,
you suggest that you should spend still another night in London,
so that you would only have one complete day here—namely
Sunday. And if I did not protest you would do this. And what
is this work? According to you it is work that 'any fool could
do', that Mrs. Dumas formerly did without assistance, and
that is at most 12 hours a week. For this, if I did not protest,
domestic life at Comarques would be reduced to a mere farce.
What do you suppose Mrs. Dumas would say if someone
suggested to her that she should be absent from her own house
except from Saturday evening to Monday afternoon in order
to do 12 hours work that 'any fool could do'? And what do
you suppose her husband would say? You would never have
dreamed of taking on such work if it had not been in London.
and given you an opportunity of staying longer in London.
If you really want to do war work, as I believe you do, you
can quite well get work on Tuesdays, Wednesdays, Thursdays,
and Fridays, if you try. I know that you prefer to be in London.
Well, you have got a flat in London and you have three days
in London. You ask for my opinion. You have it. You are,
as always, free to do what you like. And I only give you my
opinion because you ask for it. In any case, please do not talk

94

any more about closing this house. This idea is always putting me off my work, and stopping me from sleeping, and my work is quite difficult and complicated enough without that.

Je te bise,

A.B.

The work that 'any fool could do' was at a Y.M.C.A. canteen near Waterloo Station. It served soldiers going on and coming back from leave. At first she and a girl of fifteen were put onto washing-up, Saturdays only, 11 a.m. to 2.30 p.m., standing up, with nothing to refresh themselves except a quick cup of coffee. Arnold comments in his Journal : 'Women do like this exhausting work. It wears them out and then they think they have done something grand.' She was going to undertake four hours a day for three days a week until Arnold stopped her.

Any further argument about a joint flat in town ended early in May when Arnold entered upon greater responsibilities, and a new phase in his life, as Director of British Propaganda in France with a special grant of £100,000 and offices in Norfolk Street, Strand. He had been offered the job by the then Minister of Information, Lord Beaverbrook.

Mme. Arnold Bennett,   Comarques,
52, Oxford Street,   Thorpe-le-Soken.
London, W.1.   9th May, 1918.
Mon enfant chérie,

I have done my first day's work. It's not really work. To start with, a big lunch (Savoy) to allied journalists, the Minister presiding. Afterwards, I see all kinds of people, men and women, who work under my orders. There will be set-backs and jealousies, and the whole field is enormous, but all-in-all it is not what I call work, and everybody seems delighted to meet this author and dramatist !

Dinner this evening at the 'Other Club'.

Tomorrow evening I am dining with the Minister of Justice, Sir F. E. Smith.

I kiss you well,

A.

(Sir F. E. Smith was, of course, afterwards Lord Birkenhead.) Later in the month Marguérite visited the Midlands in a round of calls on friends and relations.

Mme. Arnold Bennett.   Ministry of Information.
                                        27th May, 1918.
Chérie,

Two letters from you this morning, in pencil. So it is understood that I will keep Friday evening [*for you*]. On Thursday I shall be engaged. I am indeed infinitely engaged. Yesterday I wrote you a passably long letter addressed to Congleton. I didn't think for a moment that you would leave those dear Masons before Tuesday. I am pleased that you have decided to go and see the Five Towns people. It won't be much trouble, I imagine . . .

I left the house [Comarques] this morning at 8 o'clock by bicycle. Nice morning. A little tired. I work all day here, but it's not work as I know it. I was to have had an official dinner this evening but at the last moment it was put off, thanks to the vicissitudes of the French Minister for Foreign Affairs.

So I kiss you well,
Thy Nouche.

Mme. Arnold Bennett,   Ministry of Information.
52, Oxford Street,
London, W.1.   11th June, 1918.

Mon enfant chérie,

I have received your letter. I think it is a great pity that you are not staying at Thorpe this week. You have undoubtedly been very unwell, and everyone says how ill you look. To come to London to a flat without a servant when you might stay at Thorpe must strike everybody else as a very queer thing to do. However, it is your affair.

The international situation is extremely serious. Preparations are being made to evacuate Paris. This is *most strictly private* between you and me. I know I can rely on you not to say anything.

About this time gossip began to circulate about the Bennetts being separated. I knew by intuition more than anything else that this was so, and when at last I was certain I talked to Arnold about it and claimed from him my rights as a wife to have him with me. He said that it was all imagination and added that people knew very well we spent weekends together at Comarques. Yet the tone of his voice implied : 'Good heavens, what a fool I have been ! It never occurred to me.' Still many months were to pass before the situation was to change. I had put my foot down and told him that I wanted him to come and sleep at my flat. He refused. He was very angry indeed and went so far as to threaten me with divorce. I kept calm and answered : 'Perhaps it would be more appropriate if I asked for the divorce !'

My poor husband was quite dumbfounded.

A few days later, Arnold was taken ill and called for me. He wanted then to come to Thackeray Mansions to be nursed by me. He was soon better and went back to his rooms at the Yacht Club.

Mme. Arnold Bennett, Comarques,
52, Oxford Street, Thorpe-le-Soken.
London, W.1. 6th August, 1918.

Mon enfant,

. . . Our present arrangement of living in London may not be ideal, but it was due to the war, and it suited you well enough at one time. It now happens to suit my work better than anything else could. I have an immense amount of work to do and I can only get through it by the most careful organisation. At the club I have no household worries of any kind. I am excellently served. I have no servant troubles; no food troubles; no coal troubles. Everything is done for me. I am perfectly quiet. The whole of my work is directly connected with the war. I get up at 6.30 four days a week to do it, and I do do it, but only just. I shall certainly not change my way of life until either my work stops or the war stops. I shall certainly not put myself to the bother and expense of taking a larger flat, and seeing to the furniture, and running all the risks in connection with servants, lighting, coal, etc. that people will have to run this winter in London. No fear! Why should I? Because mysterious people say that we are separated! The idea is childish. I fully admit that the arrangement is not ideal from the conjugal point of view. But there is certainly no hardship. Every free evening I spend with you. And I would certainly sooner spend an evening alone with you than in any other way!

I kiss you,

A.

Arnold Bennett Esq.,   52, Oxford Street,
Royal Thames Yacht Club.   London, W.1.
                                 7th August, 1918.

Mon chéri,

. . . As to the idea of getting a somewhat bigger home in London, I did not want to rush matters, but you will never give me a chance to discuss it. You will have your own way. You don't want a joint home in London, so you don't like me to mention it. For one thing, it's not your idea, but mine. But if you had a joint home, you wouldn't need to worry about furniture. Anybody else would recognise that your wife would be quite capable of sparing you that kind of worry. She is not altogether without tact, capacity, or experience.

I understand how much you work, but you are not the only husband to do so. The trouble is that you do as much as three clever men together. I ought to be proud of you since you are like that, and I am, but I cannot feel happy when I see you working yourself to death without me to nurse you and look after you when your day's work is done. Of course, if you had been one of the men at the front, it would have been very different. But then at least I should hear from you every day and know that I could not have you to myself.

You say that I claim far too much. It is no longer any use for me to claim anything, and you must just please yourself. But please, try to look more cheerful.

I kiss you, Nouche,

Your perpetual torment,

Marguérite.

Mme. Arnold Bennett,   Reform Club,
Comarques,   London, W.1.
Thorpe-le-Soken.   15th August, 1918.

Mon enfanta carita,

. . . It is 10.30 and I have written my Lloyd's article. Rather good. Still sleeping rottenly. An official dinner tonight. There was one on Tuesday night; a lunch yesterday; and another lunch today! Beaverbrook is away ill. I am very tired. I catch the 4.59 tomorrow, Friday.

The housekeeper at the Yacht Club told me that you had kindly approved my miserable room at the Club. If the Committee knew that she had taken you up there she would be dismissed. However, that's her affair. Nothing to do with me . . .

I kiss you, while hoping that you are better.

Nouche.

Mme. Arnold Bennett,   Ministry of Information.
52 Oxford Street,
London, W.1.   21st August, 1918

Mon enfant chérie,

I know that Walpole[1] would object to altering that dinner. In fact he could not properly alter it, nor could I refuse to go, simply because you did not want to travel by Tube to Liverpool Street. [*Liverpool Street Station is of course the London terminus for the Essex trains.*] I very greatly regret your being alone tonight, but I hope you will find some friend (to keep you company). Anyhow it is impossible for me to alter my arrangements at the last moment. How many times have you said when I was free and alone, and you weren't: 'My darling, I am sorry but I am engaged this evening.' And I have in no way insisted. It's a nuisance, but that's how it is. If you are going to be in London on Thursday or Friday evening, let me know.

I kiss you,
Nouche.

[1] Hugh Walpole, The novelist.

Mme. Arnold Bennett,   Royal Thames Yacht Club.
52 Oxford Street,
London, W.1.   27th August, 1918.

Mon enfant chérie,

. . . I have heard from the Doctor. He says that the only thing you have is bronchial catarrh, which will soon be cured. But he advises me to take another flat for you. *Although* the letter is such that you might have dictated it for him to sign and bears every evidence of a conspiracy, and *although* I shall be put to a great deal of inconvenience, and *although* I am somewhat surprised that you cannot accomplish the small sacrifice which the present state of affairs involves, I believe in following the advice of a doctor when once he has been consulted. We shall therefore have a new flat.

This flat must be central, as near to places and to clubs as possible. I shall want two rooms in it, one bedroom at the back I don't mind how small—and a room to work in which *must* be a good room. You can put your own furniture into the rest of the flat, but I must see to my 2 rooms myself entirely. It will be much cheaper in the end, so far as my work, etc., is concerned, to spend a few hundreds a year extra and get what is really comfortable than to have a few hundreds and be worried all the time. . . .

I kiss you well,
Nouche.

Oddly enough, not another word is heard from either of them on the subject of the proposed new flat for the two of them, at least for six months.

Mme. Arnold Bennett,   Ministry of Information,
52 Oxford Street,   Norfolk Street,
London, W.1.   Strand, W.C.2.
                               27.9.18

My dear Marguérite,

I enclose cheque for £20 for your birthday present.

I wish you to understand that it is *quite impossible* for me to sleep at the flat every night when I am in London. I can sleep there occasionally, and in spite of the inconveniences for me, I enjoy doing so; but I cannot do it every night, or nearly every night. I know I shall never succeed in making you understand what the working life of a man in my position is. Quite apart from my work here, and my articles, there is a multitude of daily things that are always presenting themselves to a man who has as much influence with the public as I am supposed to have, and is as well known as I am. These things *have to be attended to,* and they cannot be attended to without regular work. I have arranged for myself a study at the club where I have the necessary apparatus and where I have also the apparatus of the club to help me. The idea of doing all this in a corner of your drawing-room is impossible. The idea of my writing my articles in your drawing-room is grotesque. If you cannot appreciate this I must ask you to accept it from me, and not to accuse me of bad faith, as you did this morning. It is really very inexcusable of you to say that I don't come to live at the flat because I don't want to.

You don't seem to desire to learn that you cannot say everything that comes into your head, without trouble arising. I say nothing about the scandalous scenes you made at Comarques, because you have fully apologised for them. But really you soon forget. A few days later you were criticising me in front of Richard in the most monstrous way. I pointed this out to you at the time. No expression of regret, however! And the next day you began again. Worse, no expression of regret. When I mentioned the matter, at length, you were merely sarcastic and disagreeable. You simply said : *'Oh, je passe ma vie en retirant les choses que j'ai dit.'* [Oh, I spend my life taking back things I have said.'] I assure you that I am doing all I can for you. I cannot do more and I shall not attempt to do more. And I cannot say that I get that sympathy from you which I think I ought to have. I know that there are difficulties for you, but these difficulties have to be accepted, if they cannot be overcome. You wanted a flat in London. You chose it. You had it. You now want a change. I don't blame you for wanting a change, though I entirely disagree with you on the point; I give way. You want in the meantime to sleep at a hotel. It seems to me extraordinary—and it would seem extraordinary to most people—that a woman with two houses and a season ticket must sleep in a hotel. Still, there it is. If you want to you must. You will have difficulties. I quite sympathise with your difficulties. But I cannot help them. You are 44; you have many friends. There are certain things which you will have to see after for yourself. Everyone has serious difficulties. Everyone suffers.

I notice also, that, though you are very anxious for me to give way to you in everything, you don't show much desire to meet me half way. You know how I hate being in London at weekends, and how I like being at Comarques at weekends. I should have thought this could be organised. But you see in the project nothing but impossibilities and difficulties. The fact is that you don't want to be at Comarques at weekends. I realise that if you have made up your mind about this there is nothing further to be done, as difficulties will always occur. Comarques will therefore be closed for the winter. This I have definitely decided, and we will say no more about it. It will doubtless be necessary for you to go from time to time to see to Miss Lambert and so on, but the place will be closed. You needn't say any more about it. I am not going to have any more arguments. I am not going to have any more scenes. I seem to do little but give way to you, and that doesn't help much. I expect there is no need to repeat what I have told you in my previous letter; you accuse me of being silent. Of course I am silent. But you can soon cure my silence.

Your

A.B.

No further mention is made of Comarques being shut for the winter, and it never was so shut. Two days later Arnold was writing from the house as follows :

Mme. Arnold Bennett,	Comarques,
52 Oxford Street,	Thorpe-le-Soken.
London, W.1.	29th September, 1918.

Mon enfant,
   . . . The electricity is not functioning as Harry has made

some sort of mess with the engine. He says it was not clean : but it was working perfectly last week. However, Dummerton is putting it right. In the meantime we have to manage with lamps and candles. I haven't seen Lambert [*the new woman gardener who had replaced Lockyer while the latter was in the army*] but the garden looks very untidy—tools, cans, tins, and pairs of steps left lying about in the open. I have put them all together so that she will notice them. I expect that she is young enough to need some supervision.

I can scarcely sleep for thinking of the enormous work and the responsibilities which I now have. It seems to me impossible that I am the chief person in the Ministry, after the Minister. You said I should be, but I could not have believed it. The funniest thing of all is that at Christmas I shall be the one who recommends the various members of the staff for titles and honours! I now have three secretaries—in fact, until I get settled down, I shall have four. I hope you have arranged not to be too much alone, and not to be too bored. I have no doubt you have. And you will have recovered tomorrow. I had an enormous day yesterday. I just caught the train, and it was very empty.

I kiss you,
Nouche

P.s. I hope to arrive before 7.30 on Monday evening, but that's not certain. I shall be engaged on Tuesday evening and Thursday evening. I have arranged for (us to go to) the Ballet Russe on Wednesday evening.

Mme. Arnold Bennett,   Ministry of Information,
52 Oxford Street,   Norfolk Street,
London, W.1.   Strand, W.C.2.
       30.9.18

My child,

I have your two letters. It is no use discussing this. There is only one principal point. I will not be criticized before other people, and I will not allow anybody to do it to me. If you *really* do *not* want me to come to dinner tonight (either at the flat or at a restaurant) send word by Miss Nerney, otherwise I shall come. Unfortunately I am so extremely busy with my new situation here, that I can't attend to my own affairs.

I kiss you,
A.B.

Mme. Arnold Bennett,   The Reform Club,
52, Oxford Street,   London, W.1.
London, W.1.   24th October, 1918.

Wife,

Today I have been inundated, devastated, drowned, by work and official worries. It will continue for several days at least. Enormous changes. The Minister [*Lord Beaverbrook*] is going to have an operation tomorrow. He wrote me a letter today which I will show you later . . . This evening I have a nervous headache. Dinner later to discuss co-operation between the Admiralty and the Minister. Sir Guy Garnett and I are the two principal combatants! In the circumstances dinner is being provided by Lieut. Herbert Sullivan [*i.e. his friend from Essex*] of the Admiralty. Yesterday evening the men of the French state tired me terribly, but Painlevé[2] is very kind. You are well, I hope.

Wife, I kiss thee,
Nouche.

The war came to an end with the Armistice of 11th November. The day before this happened, with his eye on the new turn their life must take, Arnold wrote: 'I have heard of some flats, one looking over Hyde Park. But I have had the idea that I do not want a house in the country, a large flat in London, and a yacht. I have had the idea, not of selling Comarques, but of letting it unfurnished, so that we could go back to it when we are older if we want to. I want to simplify existence for the next few years as much as possible, so that we can see how events turn out.'

Nothing more is heard of letting Comarques. On 14th November he was writing: 'It seems to me very possible that if you do

[2] Paul Painlevé, mathematician and statesman, briefly French premier in 1917.

not go up to Comarques regularly each week you may have further
trouble. You have only been up twice in five weeks—unless you go
this week. When these young people (he meant the staff) are left
to themselves, they get wrong ideas into their heads. This is
notorious. I may be wrong but I think it quite possible that if
Lambert had had the benefit of your influence each week she
might still be there. However, I merely respectfully offer you my
humble opinion.'

Marguérite apparently was not in favour of letting Comarques
(her letter is lost) but she put forward another suggestion.

Mme. Arnold Bennett,   Reform Club,
52 Oxford Street,   London, W.1.
London, W.1.   16th November, 1918.

Mon enfant chérie,
    The suggestion in your letter for future arrangements is
excellent from your point of view but not from mine, as it would
make my work impossible. If you want to close Comarques for
4 months in the winter I am ready to agree, as I know you
dislike housekeeping intensely. But it would not do at all for
me to live at the club and have a room for Miss Nerney at your
flat. When Comarques was open every weekend I could manage
very well 3 days in the week alone, as I could always return to
my 'base' and my secretary for 3 or 4 days. But if I am to be
cut off from my base for four months it is essential that I
should have a new and proper base in London, and it is essential
that Miss Nerney should work in the place where I work, and
be on call all the time. If you understood the nature and com-
plexities of my work you would understand this at once. My
rooms at the Club were a war measure and depended on my
being every weekend at Comarques. I have only been able to
manage with them recently because I have not been doing my
own work and because I have had two offices, with Miss Nerney
next door to me. I am staying at the Ministry for the convenience
of having offices free of charge, together with free coal etc.
But I shall not be able to stay there later than Christmas at the
most, and then I shall have to find something else, as it is

absolutely impossible for me to do my own work and my correspondence without a lot of books and a lot of papers and Miss Nerney next door to me. I shall have to find a flat for myself and give up the Club. I am quite willing for you to arrange as you please the matters which concern your existence, but I alone can decide how my work is to be done.

I hope you understand. I would have told it all to you yesterday evening but I was too exhausted. The reception you gave me, which seemed so hostile, hard, and critical, finished me after my week's labours. Happily, after an hour you recalled what the role of wife ought to be; but during that hour you exhausted me.

I shall return on Tuesday evening.

I kiss you well,

Nouche.

But he was not to be given until Christmas to enjoy the Ministry's office and free coal; on the 14th he was writing: 'I have been able honourably to hand in my resignation! I have handed it in! And I am very pleased about it. I will tell you all the details.'

That winter he was busy picking up the threads of everyday existence. Chiefly he was occupied with writing the play *Judith* for Lillah McCarthy, but also he was engaged with the Lyric Theatre, Hammersmith, of which he was a director and where, he says, 'money has been lost in my absence'. Meanwhile he continued to lodge at the Yacht Club, and Marguérite at her flat. 'I only spoke of getting a flat of my own,' he was writing on the 18th November, 'because you said several times, and you always wrote it, that you wanted to live by yourself in London on account of your heart! I certainly don't want to live alone, and I am quite sure that it is a very bad thing for you to live alone. The idea of taking rooms in a hotel is impossible. Personally, I want to go back to Comarques as soon as possible after Christmas.'

However, a change was on the way. Periodically, when visiting France or staying at Comarques for any length of time, Marguérite had been in the habit of letting her Oxford Street flat for as long as a month. She had had trouble with some tenants called Green, and early in 1919 the flat was burgled. Arnold's letter notifying

Marguérite of the burglary is more important because it contains the first mention of George Street. This was a first-floor flat in George Street, Hanover Square, which was large and comfortable enough to serve both of them as a London house. Marguérite was on the point of gaining her ambition to live with her husband when in London.

Mme. Arnold Bennett, Royal Thames Yacht Club,
Comarques, 80, Piccadilly,
Thorpe-le-Soken. London, W.1.
7th March, 1919.

Mon enf.ch.,

When I was at the Hammersmith theatre [*the Lyric*] last night, Miss Forbes [*the tenant*] rang up and told me that the flat had been burgled and that Annie [*the maid*] was in a terrible state. However, as she told me that nothing of yours had been stolen I remained calm and returned to the performance . . . I see nothing for you to worry about. But you will doubtless look into the affair on your return, and it will be a good subject of conversation.

I haven't time to refer to your letter again now, but I seem to remember that you asked about the George Street flat. I am still negotiating with them. They say now they will include *all* the tenants' fixtures in the premium. So I am continuing. Something may be arranged . . .

Next day he was writing: 'Nothing new about the burglary at your flat, nor about the flat in George Street. But everyone tells me I ought to take that flat, even at the price asked.' He took the flat although he was not to occupy it until September. He wrote in affectionate terms on 6th June, 1919:

I was at the flat yesterday with Tom Smith and I chose new paper for the drawing-room. He said you wanted a stripe and yellow, and so I chose a yellow stripe. The ceiling is in a dreadful state, and the drawing-room looks like Ypres. I have at last stopped Daws from locking me out of the flat. They are now making a to-do about the affair of the plumber. It will have to be handled very carefully. Mr. Braby is so handling it. (*Mr. Braby was the Bennetts' solicitor.*)

I suppose I shall owe you another £12 tomorrow. I certainly do not wish to deprive you of the free use of lots of money (especially as I am earning nothing) but the new housekeeping arrangement seems to me to work out very oddly at times. You are away (*in France*) for a week, and I am paying the whole of your expenses. I am paying the whole of my own expenses. You never have to pay for vegetables or drinks etc. and yet— £12 for housekeeping and London expenses! I know you say that one must take one week with another. Even so, it is very remarkable. However.

In September, 1919, this flat, 12B, George Street, became their London home. Marguérite's flat continued to be let, and whenever possible they spent weekends and holidays at Comarques. The principal reason for Marguérite's dissatisfaction was thus removed, but domestic peace was still not to be theirs. In 'A.B. . . . a minor marginal note', Pauline Smith thus describes the atmosphere at George Street :

This brief visit to the flat, with its one quiet evening—the last, it proved, that I was to share with them both—and its friendly family breakfast for three next morning, was happier than any I had spent at Comarques in the crowded war years. Yet in spite of its peace for me, there came from M. at its close, as I bade her goodbye, the old impetuous complaint of the French-woman married to the 'so difficult' Englishman who would never understand her as one of her own race would surely understand her—a complaint through which I waited in vain for the once reassuring *mais il y a des moments* of romance in domesticity, hung ominous as a storm-bearing cloud in what had seemed to me so fair and serene and prosperous a sky.

CHAPTER XI

A Son of My Own

The question has often been asked, at least within the family, why no children were born of the marriage. The following explanation, with letters taken out of chronological order for that purpose, supplies the answer. One would dearly like to have seen Marguérite's letter to which the first extract, from Arnold, is a reply.

Marguérite   Comarques.
(by hand).   29.7.17.
. . . It is not the fact that I object to children because of my work. Far from that. I have never stated my reason, because I hate to state it. Nevertheless you ought to be clever enough to see it. My reason is that my father died of softening of the brain and was always slightly queer in his head, and that two members of your family are abnormal mentally. These things are apt to jump a generation. This reason, which I have never before mentioned to anyone, *and which I absolutely decline to discuss,* seems to me a good one . . .

This letter was placed before Marguérite's nephew and executor, M. Etienne Lombrail, who is a lawyer. He emphatically denies that any member of the Soulié family, or for that matter any members of the Hébrard or Villeneuve families, from whom Marguérite was descended, were mentally abnormal, at least within living memory. The 'softening of the brain' from which Enoch died, which is so realistically portrayed in *Clayhanger,* may medically be described as cerebral arterio-sclerosis. Two of Arnold's sisters also died of it, but it is not congenital. At least, none of the present writer's generation has suffered from it. Another explanation for Arnold's objection to children may be found in a conversation recorded by his eldest sister, Sissie. 'Children!' Arnold told her. 'True, I have no children. I have no use for them. They do not enter into my horizon for they upset the easy-running of a house. Moreover, it is not as if children were toys that can be put away in a cupboard when one tires of them.'

Be that as it may, Marguérite had taken care of Richard Bennett, Frank's eldest son (Frank, it will be remembered, was the solicitor in Rochdale) since he was a small boy. Until the Adoption of Children Act came into force in 1926, children were the inalienable responsibility of their parents. To get over this, and bind Richard more securely to them, Marguérite conceived the notion of changing Richard's name, whether to Richard Arnold Bennett or simply to Arnold Bennett does not emerge.

Marguérite   Comarques.
(by hand).   7th August, 1918.

Mon enfant,

. . . As regards legal adoption I told you when we took Richard that there is *no such thing* as legal adoption in England. There is in almost all other countries, but not in England. Nothing that we could do legally would bind either Richard or us in the slightest degree. Our hold on Richard will depend solely on the way we treat him.

Mme. Arnold Bennett,   Royal Thames Yacht Club,
Comarques.   80, Piccadilly,
                                 London, W.1.
                    17th September, 1917.

Mon enfant,

In order to oblige you I don't mind paying for *the alterations* of your will (which will be quite simple) but I do not think that it would be at all 'fair' that I should pay for a document [*i.e. that relating to the changing of Richard's name*] to which I strongly objected, which was made in defiance of me, and which has caused me a large amount of discomfort and worry.

You say that you have the right to express a wish. That may or may not be so. But it is absolutely certain that you have not the right to desire the boy, in a formal and solemn document, to do a public act which you know must cause me intense pain and annoyance. That was an outrage.

You say that my name is yours. That may be so, but it remains at least as much my property as yours. You cannot properly ask a third person to do something with property which belongs also to another unless you first obtain the consent of that other person. In married life if a course of conduct is suggested which affects both parties, the consent of both parties must be obtained to it. Otherwise no action should take place. If one insists on defying the other in a mutual matter, he or she must accept the risks and the resulting friction.

I know how much it has cost you to give up an impossible position. This is not, as you think, a 'victory' for me. It is a victory for your commonsense over your impulsiveness.

If as you say your point in taking Richard [*i.e. in bringing him up*] no longer exists, it is a pity that you did not say before we took him that your only object was to get him to alter his name to mine. We should then have cleared that matter up at once. But you never mentioned it to me in any form. You first mentioned it to a solicitor, and told me afterwards. I should never have agreed to it at any time, however, as it would be exactly contrary to my principles.

No one knows better than you that you don't always have to give in.

When you have had your will altered, by means of a short codicil, tell the solicitors to send the bill to me. I shall come home tomorrow evening, Tuesday, towards 6.30, in any case before 7.

I kiss you and I love you,
Nouche.

Arnold Bennett Esq.,   52, Oxford Street,
Comarques.   London, W.1.
                                    18th September, 1917.

My dear Arnold,

My mind is not at peace and never will be until I write the letter I tried to write yesterday. I might have dropped the

111

matter but it would have been useless. I cannot sleep, I cannot eat, I am miserable, so once more you have to listen to my explanations, if only so that you don't have to suffer my old troubles of faintness, lack of sleep, etc. Like you I am sensitive, like you I must have everything clear. I have already told you that your clever letters don't help me in the least. They only serve to make me hysterical or angry, or merely indifferent. I mean those letters which are more like a charge by the prosecution than anything else. Just let me explain how unjust I think you have been.

I have always had the idea that if we had a child I should have loved him to bear your name, and when we had considered different ways by which we could adopt Richard, and dismissed them, I secretly, jealously, and lovingly cherished this ambition —a very tiny ambition—which would please and flatter all husbands—except my own. When one has a child, or adopts a child, one must think of his future, provide funds for him, give him an education—one must also give him a name when this name means something that will ultimately benefit him.

Now, without wishing to talk like a snob, but talking with the commonsense that you yourself recognise—you are the first member of your family to make a name for himself. By your industry, your genius, and perhaps with my help, you have transformed this name so that it has become not just 'Bennett' but 'Arnold Bennett'. You are Mr. Arnold Bennett, and I am known as Mrs. Arnold Bennett. Are there not all sorts of reasons why Richard, the son whom I chose to adopt *with your consent,* should not bear our name? Not a single friend, male or female, would blame us. You condemn this idea of mine. My dear Arnold, don't you think that perhaps you are considering only your own feelings and not mine?

If only at the start of this affair you had made yourself perfectly clear! No! When with great trepidation I had plucked up courage to tell you what was in my mind, you smiled as though flattered and you said : 'But you can't change a name like that!' I answered : 'But yes, it's done everyday.' To that you made no reply. You can't deny it.

What you won't admit is that you are now pretending to forget our talk in the train so that you can humiliate me. I had

Marguérite 1920

Grand Hôtel, Finsterwald
10 Août '81

Ma chère...

Il me semble que je suis bien simple. Je ne sais pas où trouver les arguments curieux que tu as... Si ce n'est pas le siècle... C'est des allusions que je fais sur les choses auxquelles on veut choisir, ou mystérieuses...

Si tu crois que c'est drôle pour une femme de se sentir depuis près de 14 ans une enfant méchante ou capricieuse, ou mystérieuse, un être qui aurait dû dépuis longtemps partir définitivement et devenir un été à ton visage — ça arrive!

prends pas une ombre d'espoir les choses qui me rendent si mystérieuse à ta...

Je t'en prie sois heureux, ne te tourmente pas.

C'est avec plaisir sur l'affiche que tu as su faire connaissance d'aucun musical comedy actors. Elles ont défini les femmes que tu as choisies d'as la chair. Je les tiens aussi sérieusement que tu tiens les amis heureux qui as autres...

Je t'embrasse à jamais...

Photo by Kimrov

decided never again to raise this question, but the other day you came into my boudoir and saw the solicitor's bill on my desk. Now you pretend that you had instructed me to change the will, when you know very well that I had decided not to change a word of what I had drafted. You make me out to be a wife so guilty that you can never forgive her. What you really mean is that you will never try to understand the mysterious promptings of her heart.

The other day I was re-reading some of your letters and the crimes that in the past you have charged me with. They are so innumerable that I wonder how it is you have managed to live so long with such a wife. I have always had to yield. I know that I shall always have to yield, but, my dear, do you realise that my love has vanished in the course of yielding? All last winter I struggled to make you remember that you had a wife. I wanted to prove my affection for you—my love; but I failed except to satisfy your desire, and then only when your work was not interrupted. You remember the whole series of letters that passed between us before you would agree to spend just one regular evening with me per week.

That phrase in your last letter, 'I love you', moves me because I know what it costs you to write it. I love you still—but I beg you to take care because indifference is filling my heart, which has had enough of suffering.

Before I finish, I must mention that since I promised not to speak when others were present, all conversation in the house has dried up. Sometimes I feel utterly frustrated when, among friends and strangers, I am obliged to hold my tongue so as not to contradict you or in any way cross your wishes. If only you would try not to endow me with a character I don't possess!

You are bound to write me a long letter destroying everything I hold dear. I have made up my mind not to read your reply. I shall be satisfied only to learn that you have read this letter.

I shall stay in London unless you have need of me at Comarques. I hope I shan't find that you have been smitten with some terrible illness, although if this happens you know all too well that you can count on me to nurse you. We ought to be very, very happy, you and I, to which end I beg you to try not to be so demanding and severe. Make some effort, however small, to show me that you love me, that I don't serve only to make you suffer.

Let me repeat that I have ceased to care about Richard's future. You have killed that ambition. Well, so be it.

I wish to have a son of my own.

Your unreasonable wife,
Marguérite.

CHAPTER XII

The Poetry Recitals

To instruct, to point out how the human lot might be improved, was as instinctive with Arnold as it was with his brothers and sisters. It is not by chance that he most commonly began his letters to Marguérite with *Mon enfant,* nor that a series of instructive booklets came from his pen, as for example, *How to Live on 24 Hours a Day, The Human Machine,* and *Literary Taste: How to Form It.* In 1920 he was bringing the weight of his authority and experience to bear on the subject of woman and marriage in a booklet called: *Our Women: Chapters on the Sex-Discord,*[1] and in 1921 he republished an earlier booklet called *Married Life: The Plain Man and his Wife.*[2]

However informed and persuasive these manuals may be, their author was forbidding his own wife to speak while others were present, or to voice criticism of him; he was living apart from her while expecting her to nurse him, sleep with him, and keep his country house when required; he was leaving angry four-page letters on her dressing-table because, for example, she had shut some folding-doors and moved the piano. Nor was she just any wife, a meek Mrs. Charles Dickens or a kind-hearted Mrs. John Galsworthy—she was a stylish Frenchwoman who loved the drama of life, who very often acted impulsively and sometimes with violence, and in the absence of children found fulfilment in giving recitals of French poetry. This authority on married life had rarely, if ever, taken his wife with him purely because he enjoyed her company: in February, 1920, for example, he took a long leisurely cruise to Portugal in the R.M.S. *Hildebrand,* but he didn't take Marguérite. He took his friend and disciple, Frank Swinnerton, the novelist.

What he was doing in effect was to deny her the right to exist as an individual and leasing her out at so much a month, something even less than the 'married mistress' she claimed he made of her. (What an exquisite sentence to write to one's wife: 'You say that you have the right to express a wish. That may or may

---

[1] Cassell. Previously serialised in *Cassell's Magazine.*
[2] Hodder & Stoughton, 1913.

not be so!') In her Journal Marguérite quoted the following about *Our Women*: 'My husband's book, *Our Women*, has created a sensation. The *Star* goes as follows: "A man, but not an artist, will often sacrifice everything for a woman . . . but an artist will seldom sacrifice his art for a woman. He will much more probably employ her, with an astounding ruthlessness, in the service of his art. A woman has no greater rival that the art of the artist, and the jealousy between one woman and another is mild in comparison with the jealousy which may animate a woman against the art of the artist who has captured her. Indeed, artists are in a unique position of advantage—their detachment is terrifying."

Here are some of Marguérite's own ideas on marriage scattered through her Journal:

23rd September, 1920.
My husband hardly ever agrees with me when I suggest something I want to do—we don't seem to see things in the same way and this makes me miserable and hurts me because of his sarcasms. He will never tell me of his arrangements or what he is going to do about anything. It sounds so strange to me when I believe that it is only natural to have no secrets at all from one's husband. Above all, marriage ought to be a partnership.

25th September, 1920.
He wanted to have the upper hand because he believed that our happiness would be greater if he were the unquestioned master. Though perhaps he never realised it, I had an influence over him which has made him less autocratic, not so hard and matter of fact, and not so absorbed in his artistic and financial ambitions. Yet he is still very obdurate. He will never change his mind even when he knows that he should do so. He will never admit that he is wrong.

13th March, 1921.
I married him with the main idea that I should share his mode of life. I am myself as he is, a mixture of happiness, courage, and misery. I have all the shortcomings of the human race but

116

I do know that life has made me as enduring as anyone could be, and as generous as many, and as hard as many a man if I want to be; I am as broadminded and as understanding as anyone can hope to be, and as such I am capable of taking an active part in our married life as a real companion to my husband.

By way of relief or compensation for her unhappiness she resumed those poetry recitals which she had given up early in their acquaintance. Like many another woman married to a man of strong character, she imitated him. She kept a journal, she studied Marcus Aurelius, she tried her hand at water-colours, and she even wrote an unpublished novel. But in this one medium she was unique and indeed remarkable. Arnold had already written to her as follows (in June, 1919):

I hope you have thoroughly digested what I told you about your recitations. You are not to talk as if you were talking to intimates in a salon. You are speaking to a public. You ought really to speak to the people in the last row of seats at the back. Your famous whispered last lines are lost except on the people close to you. It is very effective to drop your voice before the end of a sentence, and to murmur little remarks—asides—if you have the listener at your elbow. But before an audience these things do harm, not good. Your interpretations of the poems are believe me, masterly; they are about perfect. But they cannot wholly succeed if half the audience has to strain its ears to catch what you say, and even so misses a lot of words. All this is elementary—and of the highest importance. It is essential that you should show that you have realised the difference between a drawing-room and a hall. Of course, the conditions at the Scala house are appalling. Hence all the more need to make oneself a public *performer*.

Upon which, I kiss you well, while hoping that your headaches have completely disappeared. Nouche.

In a leaflet Marguérite advertised that she had been trained by professors from the Conservatoire and the Comédie Française,

117

and had worked under M. Lugné-Poë at the Théâtre de l'Oeuvre. In 1920 the Anglo-French Poetry Society was formed with Arnold as president and a managing committee composed of Marguérite, Edith Sitwell, and Helen Rootham[3] : under its auspices she gave recitals at the Bedford College for Women, Lindsey Hall, London, Nottingham University, and before the Franco-Scottish Society in Glasgow. Edith Sitwell wrote to her on the 17th June, 1920 : 'Never have I heard your voice in better form. It was a triumph. I assure you the audience was overwhelmed.' In this sphere she was, as Arnold had told her, masterly.

Marguérite's Journal   August 1920

Edith Sitwell and Helen Rootham were most impressed by the unquestionably great success of the first meeting of the A.F.P.S. which took place at our flat in George Street. All our members were delighted and expressed their satisfaction in having joined the Society. St. John Ervine was one of these people. He said to me : 'Mrs. Bennett, when you first wrote asking me to join, I must admit that I hesitated . . . but now I am so glad . . . what I enjoyed most of all was your beautiful recitation.' St. J.E. is an artist and a drama critic. Mr. de la C., whom I met for the first time, expressed his pleasure and his thanks. He added (and I was most surprised and flattered) that 'Sarah Bernhardt used her voice wonderfully and your voice is just as beautiful. You are inspired when you use it.'

I know that in spite of a bad cold, my voice was all right and my emotions true. I also know that P.L.'s remark was quite justified when he said, 'You made the same mistake three times in your pronunciation of "calme". You made the "c" sound like a "k" in the English way . . . which is unpardonable.' An English friend, Mrs. P., sad, 'Look here, my dear, you must have worked hard for years, and what a memory !'

Arnold told me that Haidee Wright (the actress) had been much impressed and greatly moved. Stella Clark recited five English poems we had selected together very well. I am very

[3] At one time Edith Sitwell's governess, Helen Rootham continued to live with her as companion. She translated Rimbaud's *Illuminations*.

proud of her. What I had foreseen happened—poetry was the most popular item of the evening, eclipsing the musical side of the programme.

Those who knew anything about decor were very struck by the way we had succeeded in achieving the right decoration and lighting. I had hired sixty seats from Harrods, and Harvey, our waiter, and myself did all the arranging of the room. [*Harvey, by the way, was much more than a 'waiter' : he was Arnold's valet.*] P.L. helped us with the lighting. Certainly A.B.'s study lends itself very well to the purpose of a recital room. The evening was a resounding success. Edith Sitwell looked magnificent in a glittering dress of gold and silver. Stella Clark looked very sweet in a blue silk dress. As for myself, I wore a dress which, I was told, was perfectly suited to the occasion. It was of white brocade, satin, and silver and gold with Egyptian tulle veils embroidered with silver. It had long sleeves like wings. It was indeed the very dress to wear for expressing the pure simplicity of the poems. I had made a selection from Ronsard, Baudelaire, Verlaine, and Francis James. It follows that all my accessories were in white satin to complete my attire. A.B. said that everything was perfect, Helen Rootham said that I was very lovely to look at, and P.L. said that everybody admired my dress.

I was told that my husband had welcomed everyone in a most charming manner. As for me, I waited in the sitting-room with my partners so as to feel quite in the mood for the evening. At the end of the recital a few friends joined us and the artists in some refreshments served in the drawing-room, which was lavishly decorated with flowers. Sir Nigel Playfair [*a co-director, with Arnold, of the Lyric Theatre, Hammersmith*] our chairman, was most entertaining and also most delighted that all our efforts had been such a success. A.B. was beaming with satisfaction. The programme was, if anything, too short—so was the evening!

With the initials "P.L." first mention is made of a man who was to have increasing influence on Marguérite. He was René Pierre Legros, a lecturer in French at the Bedford College for Women, who had been introduced to the Bennetts by Robert

Nichols, the poet. At this time M. Legros was thirty years old (Marguérite herself was forty-six), the son of a teacher in a State School in Brittany, shortish, with a small moustache, and dark deep eyes. Marguérite, an expert in diction, often remarks on the beauty of his voice. M. Legros was the current tenant of Marguérite's flat in Thackeray Mansions.

Even with the wealth of evidence now available, much of which is to follow, his exact relationship with Marguérite must remain open to question, although the response of a childless, disillusioned, and largely idle wife to a sympathetic admirer of her own nationality, one moreover who was recognised as a ladykiller, would seem to be fairly predictable. The following are extracts from Marguérite's Journal, but we must not forget that this Journal was written (or more probably improved upon) long after the events which they describe.

1st October, 1920

P. came back from his holiday in France this morning at 11.45. Annie [*the maid*] and I were expecting him. I had to send a wire to A.B. and was making for the Post Office when I ran across P.L. in the street . . . He looked very happy to be back, but tired. I feel a kind of motherly affection for him and am very sorry for him. He needs sympathy and encouragement. His nerves are all on edge. He can't help it if he is so interested in girls, but it is very bad for him to burn the candle at both ends. He often chafes under my influence and I have to be patient. He is a victim of the strain of war on his nervous system. Who knows what might have become of him if, with my husband's approval, I had not undertaken to look after him?

3rd October, 1920

. . . P.L. paid a call on A.B. this afternoon and gave him a present, five books nicely bound. Arnold is very pleased. He looked delighted to have received such a present, and P.L. was pleased to have delighted him . . . Arnold insisted that P.L. should stay to dinner. We offered him champagne and gave him advice about his health. I was so pleased to see the two get on so well together, although neither of the same generation nor nationality.

. . . An invitation (came) for us both from P.L. to dine at Thackeray Mansions. A.B. knows about my arrangement with P.L. and has indicated that he does not approve of such an understanding. I shall be only too glad to get rid of the flat as things are and I have already offered it to two of our friends, Davray[4] and Frank Swinnerton, on the same terms as those enjoyed by P.L. Neither would accept. In the meantime I am very pleased that the flat is occupied by a friend. I told A.B. that I hoped that P.L., when he is on holiday, would let me use his flat [*i.e. her flat, at Thackeray Mansions*] for studying my poems, etc., and he replied: 'Of course he will.' I feel that Arnold wishes me to do anything I like with the flat, even though he does not approve of my arrangements with P.L.

16th October, 1920

Last night we had dinner at P.L.'s—Jane H. G. Wells and we two were the only guests. Excellent plain meal. A.B. had worked at his desk all day long and was very tired, especially as he had not taken his usual afternoon rest. P. was rather uneasy about A.B., but he (A.B.) felt quite at home and installed himself in the cosiest chair in the sitting-room close to the fire. We spent a very nice evening indeed, although it was spoilt a little by a very strong electric light. This was Arnold's wish as he loves a well lighted room. Women on the whole do not. We left at 10.30 p.m.

As on every Sunday morning, P.L. took me for a long walk in Hyde Park. This pleases my husband as he has no time to accompany me for a walk. We talked a great deal about different things, my work, his work, poetry, literature, etc. P. is most entertaining.

20th October, 1920

. . . I am thinking about P.'s love affairs. I wish he would make up his mind to marry. It would be the best thing for him. I told

4 Henri Davray. French journalist and translator, a friend of their Paris years.

him so but he hates the idea. To him, marriage is to lose one's liberty. He seems to hate any form of servitude, and marriage brings with it many responsibilities. Some people are incapable of coping with them or tolerating them. P. is one of these people, I think.

31st Otober, 1920.

Somehow I get the feeling that Arnold is jealous of P. My husband always pretends that he does not know what jealousy is, and claims that he is never jealous, never has been, and never will be. At lunch time we talked about P. and A.B. said to me, 'He is a lucky man.' He meant, 'to know you'. My husband ought to be very content that I have such an interesting friend, in fact he has said so. A.B. is well aware of the influence to the good I may have on that gifted young man, and I can't help suspecting also that Arnold realises that it is a good thing that I have P. for company. After all, I see so little of Arnold because he is so seldom in, even for meals.

Perhaps with Marguérite's growing interest in M. Legros in mind, Arnold encouraged her to give a series of recitations in Scotland. At this time Arnold himself had just started his latest novel, *Mr. Prohack.*

Marguérite's Journal—18th November, 1920

My first recital took place at the MacLean Hall, Glasgow. I was not pleased with myself as I did not put why whole heart into the interpretations. Dr. Baird Smith told me that I was quite a success and the public was delighted. I consider that it was due mainly to my technique. Mr. Martin, a professor of French, said : 'Madame, in one hour you have taught my pupils more about the poetic rhythm of French verse than I have taught in many lessons.'

There is no gaiety in this hotel. It would do me good to have Pierrot (Legros) and André Gide here with Valéry Larbaud and my other French friends. I found a letter from A.B., and

Pierrot sent me a short message expressing his joy that 'le maître' [Arnold] has asked him to the first night of the new production of *Milestones* and to dinner with him at the Garrick. He adds that he is to lunch with Arnold at the Reform. He is afraid that my husband might get tired of him. He might well, one day.

Arnold Bennett Esq.,   Caledonian Station Hotel,
12B George Street,   Princes Street,
Hanover Square,   Edinburgh.
London, W.1.   Friday, 19th November, 1920.

Mon chéri,
   No letter from you since my leaving London. I know you are occupied and happy, so I am not worried.
   I wrote you after the Glasgow recital. You can imagine that I lack enthusiasm. It's not funny to have nobody near to support me. I feel rather like an oyster left behind on the sea-shore, lacking nourishment and waiting for a tide that is late in coming back. There is neither sun, nor joy, nor the presence of friends around me, and this last is what I miss most. However, I prefer solitude to the company of strangers.

Mrs. Arnold Bennett,   12B, George Street,
Palace Hotel,   Hanover Square,
Aberdeen.   London, W.1.

Ma chérie enfant,
   It's a nuisance that you weren't pleased with your first recital. I have always told you that you are too difficult (to please). You don't say whether there was much money about or not, and if you gave the third part or not. In short, I wait for details. As for me, I am not well . . . Chill. Cold theatre $3\frac{1}{2}$ hours yesterday. I got up, then went back to bed. In the end I got up at 3 p.m. . . .

I kiss you tenderly,
Nouche.

Arnold Bennett Esq.,   Caledonian Station Hotel,
12B, George Street,   Edinburgh.
Hanover Square,
London, W.1.   20th November, 1920.

Ma chérie,

... Your second letter would have worried me if I hadn't had
your wire this morning telling me that the *Milestones* rehearsal
was a great success. I was thinking of you a great deal yesterday
evening. It was a good idea to invite Bertie (Herbert Sullivan)
and Pierrot. I know that they get on well together and have a
very sincere admiration and affection for you.

How are you? That terrible chill? It might be a good precaution to go back to the theatre armed with a blanket and
hot-water bottle . . . You are right, I am too difficult. After
all, my recital at Glasgow was a huge success! Only I (and
Mr. Richmond, a little) wasn't entirely satisfied. There were
too many people. The room was too hot and Mr. Richmond
had tired me all day and I wasn't able to do justice to myself.
Yesterday, everything went much better. My recital at the
University was a real triumph.

I hope to heaven that you are well. I am happy to have left
Ingram (*the maid*) with you because she is so good and devoted
. . . Good luck this evening. I should love to be near you, in
your box.

I kiss you well, my very dear one,
Thy Marguérite.

Mme. Arnold Bennett,   12B, George Street,
Palace Hotel,   Hanover Square,
Aberdeen.   London, W.1.
                                        20th November, 1920.

My poor sweet child,

I was so desolated to get your letter from Edinburgh this
morning and to learn that you hadn't received any letters . . . I
need not tell you that I have written to you every day. I expect
that your recital yesterday gave you more satisfaction and that
your mood is now less gloomy. Of course, all this professional

124

travelling and staying in hotels and seeing strangers is awful.
But it is the price artists have to pay when they travel pro-
fessionally. For 2 hours of triumph they pay 22 hours of bore-
dom, discomfort and depression. I can tell you one thing, that
it will be much worse in America. However, it is all experience
for you, and it is part of the career, and I have no doubt that
you will survive it brilliantly.

I kiss you well and I give you courage,
Nouche.

Mme. Arnold Bennett, Palace Hotel, Aberdeen.	12B, George Street, Hanover Square, London, W.1. 21st November, 1920.

Mon enfant chérie,

I hope that you are more pleased with your recital at Edinburgh, and that you are less depressed. All the same, how
bored you must be this week-end! Anyway, in six days you will
be coming home. *Milestones* last night was a great success. I was
in a box with Bertie and Legros, but I left when the curtain
fell. I had Legros yesterday to lunch at the Reform, and to
dinner at the Garrick. And he was much impressed. I didn't
sleep too well, but I am all right.

My child, I kiss you well and await your return.
Nouche.

Marguérite's Journal—23rd November, 1920

My recital took place yesterday in the Green Room of the
Imperial Hotel, [Edinburgh], as they had not asked in good
time for a room at the University—there were lots of people
in the room and in the passages. Many had to stand. They
managed to build a kind of stage for me and I asked that they
should put a screen up where I could rest during the intervals.

The recital lasted one hour including the short breaks. People
coughed during the intervals but became respectfully silent
during the poems. At the end of the recital one of the University

125

Professors speaking French fluently thanked me on behalf of my public. He said, 'Not only has Mrs. Arnold Bennett delighted us with her presence and her Comédie Française technique, but she has also shown us that the way we read or recite poetry is no less than an assassination.'

Letter from Arnold. I am inclined to think that it is stupid of me to worry so much about him as I do. I am making a mistake no doubt when, at times, I can't help thinking that he tries to make me feel that I am neglecting him for my art— have I not been sacrificed to his art time and time again for years and years?

Extracts from Marguérite's Journal—29th November, 1920.

I came back from my tour of Scotland on the morning of Saturday the 27th November . . . A.B. was still in bed when I got back to George Street. He had had a bad night. He is still very tired and keeps on saying so. He told me that he was not the philosopher he had been, and that he would murder me if I prevented him from getting on with his work as he should. . . .

After dinner Arnold asked me to read aloud a few pages of my Journal. I read for about half an hour. He advises me to have it bound. I said to him that it was not worth while because of my handwriting. 'No doubt it's bad,' he said, 'but you know that it is worth while having it bound.'

The Journal was never bound, but subsequently it was rendered into good English and typed by Mr. David R. Clarke, now of King's College, London, who visited Marguérite in the south of France in 1956.

2nd December, 1920.

Very kindly Arnold wrote out the draft of a business letter for me to copy and send to an American literary agent about the recitals of poetry I would like to make there. A.B. does not approve of the idea that I should have a male secretary to support me on my tour, lecturing on the poetry I would interpret in public. Arnold does not seem to be willing to find even a woman for such a post. I must admit that the idea of touring America alone, while exciting, is one of intimidation.

12th December, 1920.

P.L., as on every Sunday, came round to accompany me on a walk this morning, but the snow prevented us from taking a stroll in Hyde Park. We sat by the fire instead.

15th December, 1920.

I visited an art exhibition this morning at the Burlington Club. I asked P. to come along with me. Coming back we met my husband in the street as he was going to the Reform Club for lunch. I made P. stay to lunch with me, and A.B. returned to the flat and had tea with us. I noticed that, contrary to his usual self, he was far from nice to P. He left us after tea without even saying goodbye to him. This pained me. It really is rather curious that A.B. is always perfectly charming to my new friends but generally ends by getting tired of them and doing his best to get rid of them. It indicates a certain jealousy in him. He has even been jealous of my dogs!

I am less tired and worried than I have been for some time. my voice is not so edgy and is less impatient. In fact it has changed considerably. People are bound to notice it.

Mme. Arnold Bennett,   12b George Street,
Comarques,   Hanover Square,
Thorpe-le-Soken.   London, W.1.
                                  31st December, 1920.

My dear child,

Read this letter with calmness. I write it because you alone, of all the people I have known, will not permit me to finish my sentences. I know that you are so impulsive that you cannot help it; but the fact remains. Also I will not have any scenes with you. There will be no more scenes between you and me. This is one of my periodical sermons and is very well meant.

127

You spent 1 hour 25 minutes last night in telling Canoodle-Canoodle (her pet name for Arnold) that 'no one has a right to interfere with the artist,' and that you needed help and encouragement, and that I was a stone-wall, and that it was a great shame. You said this about 20 times, until I pointed out that I had done everything to help you. You then stopped. The whole tirade was a deliberate attack on me, and I much object to it. Do not say, as usual : *'Nous ne nous comprendrons jamais.'* The comprehension is perfect. It is merely a question of justice and truth. I *have* helped and encouraged your reciting in every way. I *have* thoroughly understood your point of view and sympathised with it, and said so again and again. I have also again and again paid for your recitals. When I said positively that I thought it would be a very great mistake to take Legros to America I also said that you were free to act as you liked. You then insisted that I should ask Legros to go. This I shall never do. But I am not 'interfering with the artist'. I am giving the artist a free hand. The artist is trying to interfere with me.

This is the stort of thing I get after I have done everything possible to help and encourage you. Pardon me if I suggest that in the future I shall pay for no more recitals, and I shall begin to help and encourage you again in your work when you have expressed regret for the entirely unjust attack of last night. Not before.

I must also give you a hint that you treat me generally with increasing rudeness. On Wednesday, though I was in for lunch, you went out for lunch without saying a word to me, and when you came back you made no reference of any kind to your absence. I do *not* say you ought always to tell me where you have been for lunch. Certainly not. You are perfectly entitled to go where you like and to tell me, or not tell me, as you prefer. But you are not entitled, and *no* one is entitled—least of all the mistress of the house—to absent yourself from meals without a word of warning before or a word of explanation afterwards. To do so is extremely rude, and it is rude whether you are ill or whether you are well. Two days before that, in the morning, someone rushed into my study to get the key to the brandy because Madame was unwell. I came short(ly) afterwards to see how you were. You had gone out. You returned towards 7

128

Arnold's letter to Marguérite, 5th December 1909 (translated in part on pp. 42-43)

tendrement at the end of the voyage

and am * * * * * * your

most affectionate husband

A characteristic signature

Photo Howard Coster

Arnold Bennett c. 1923

o'clock. You were out the whole day, but you never offered a word as to your absence. It has happened to me, this autumn, to have tea by myself here *every day for a whole week*. And only on one day did you give the slightest hint as to where you had been. I say again that you are entitled to this silence, and this mystery, and these absences. But a certain moderation and discretion is advisable in these matters. Whereas I tell you everything that I do, you do not tell me as often as once a fortnight what you do. Once or twice some months ago I asked you, but the replies I received were so evasive and so *'hargneux'* (peevish) that I did not ask any more. This behaviour is unwise. Almost once a fortnight you say casually that you have been to Legros' flat, but that is all. You like to pretend that I am jealous of Legros. It flatters you to think so. But it is not true. I am incapable of being jealous, probably because I should regard a woman capable of doing anything deserving of jealousy as not worth being jealous about. My behaviour to Legros has always been extremely cordial and nice. No fault can be found with it. You know this. He knows it. No man who was jealous could treat Legros as I treat him. So far as I am concerned you are absolutely free to go and see any men you like in their own *garçonière,* and to leave me alone. Few husbands would say this. No French husband would say it. Even the admirable Georges [Bion] would not say it. But I say it. You yourself would be ferociously sarcastic about any other woman who does as you do, and you would call her husband a fool. But my ideas are fairly broad. I am rather fond of you, and I have no doubts of you. At the same time, perfect freedom should not lead you into exaggeration. And, above all, it should not lead you into being constantly rude to your husband by neglecting the elementary politeness which is due to him.

As regards presents, do you not agree that present-giving should be not a duty but a pleasure? To give to one whose behaviour is constantly wounding is not a very keen pleasure. I think that when you have realised what is due to me and acted accordingly, you will not go short of presents. All sensible people must regret to hear you say, as you often do: *'I am determined to think only of myself and to do exactly what I like.'*

They regret it, because it sounds so very queer from a student of Marcus Aurelius, and because such a line of conduct always has led and always will lead, to unhappiness. You are in danger of making a fool of yourself with your husband. Don't do it. Your husband is worth caring for and worth treating perfectly. He is also very strong and very clever and his affection will not lead him into excusing too much. I can excuse a lot on the ground of ill-health and nerves; I do. But not all. And do not make the mistake of thinking you are a *femme incomprise*. You aren't, at any rate by me.

Ton mari.

(By hand to Arnold
at 12ʙ George Street.)

12ʙ George Street,
Hanover Square,
London, W.1.
2nd January, 1921.

Mon chéri,

Thank you for your letter of the 31st December. At first I thought it necessary to reply point by point; then I told myself that you knew better than I the pros and cons.

I must insist that I never had any intention of 'being rude to you'. I am sorry.

Did I truly say that you were not encouraging me in my art? . . . it's unimaginable. I thought I only talked about America. I suppose that instinctively I was trying to find out if your ideas on the subject were still the same. All these crises are hard and painful to us both.

As I told you yesterday evening (and you agreed) I have taken the decision, for both our sakes, to go away for some weeks three times a year—in January, April, and August. I also want to get back into the habit I had when we came to London, of knowing that I can keep one full evening a week to myself. Either Wednesday or Saturday will do—I will choose the one that suits you best. My absences will be easy to explain to everybody. You will please me by putting into writing that you agree. We shall thus avoid shocks and surprises.

We become irritated when we share the same surroundings. If we don't want to waste our energy and happiness in clashes of personality, whether open or concealed, it is high time to find a remedy.

I don't doubt that you will see the wisdom and affection that oblige me to make a decision which, up to now, I have not had the courage to make.

Thank you for having written to me. I am sorry to have caused you sorrow.

I embrace you tenderly,
Thy wife, Marguérite.

(How the foregoing letter came back into Marguérite's possession can only be conjectured. Unlike some of her other letters, it is neither a draft nor a copy but the original.)

Marguérite   12B, George Street,
(by hand).   Hanover Square,
London, W.1.
5th January, 1921.

My dear child,

Thank you for your letter, which I appreciate. I am glad that you see my point of view, and I was also glad to hear you say that, in growing older, I have become more kind. You speak of differences of temperament, but the matters which I complained of had nothing to do with differences of temperament. They are matters of ordinary politeness, justice, and discretion; which qualities are equally obligatory upon all temperaments, if organised society is to continue to be possible.

You cannot possibly be more free in the future than you have been in the past, but as you wish me to say that I agree to your having Wednesday evening in each week free and entirely to yourself, and also to your taking 3 holidays a year without me, I say that I agree to the same with pleasure and goodwill.

I kiss you well,

Thy husband.

The above was left on Marguérite's dressing-table, as usual, and on the envelope in her handwriting are the words: *'Très important'*. One can understand why she thought it important: the trip to the States with Legros was never again mentioned, but she might now meet him elsewhere.

Marguérite's Journal—23rd March, 1921

I left London on the 6.45 evening train for Paris.

A.B. came to Victoria to see me off. He asked me what I had done all day, and said that he had had lunch with T.M. while Miss Nerney had telephoned P.L. to find out his address in

France. 'Do you propose to write to him?' I asked. 'Possibly,' was his answer, and I retorted in English : 'Don't worry, everything is for the benefit of both of us.' We kissed goodbye and he left me five minutes before the train started. He looked quite pleased with himself and very smart with a red carnation in his button-hole, balancing himself as he walked, as he always does when he is feeling satisfied.

Marguérite's Journal—29th March, 1921

I have nearly finished *Sacred and Profane Love* and am revising (my interpretation of) a Ballade by François Villon—*La Ballade des Dames du Temps Jadis*. Strange that I find I can stay here (San Remo) doing nothing at all, just dreaming. It is as if some mysterious physical reason were at the root of such apathy.

I am told that Rome is surrounded by villages with quite comfortable hotels. I don't dislike a bit of adventure, so I will risk Rome all by myself.

Arnold Bennett Esq.,   Grand Hotel,
12B, George Street,   Frascati.
Hanover Square,
London, W.1.   1st April, 1921.

Mon grand chéri,

You would love it here. We must come some day. The town is interesting . . . not crowded with strangers. There are two cafés, very simple, wide streets well paved. The busy quarters are extremely interesting. Life here is very primitive. The shopkeepers have their shops in a kind of cellar. I wonder how the cobblers, the carpenters, the bakers, the blacksmiths manage to see. Their only light penetrates a vast archway into the holes they work in.

Women and children are everywhere. Life is tranquil. Faces are peaceful, not those of beasts as in other countries. A market is held every day. A real Italian market where vegetables and dried fruit are sold. I allowed myself to be tempted by some dried figs. 100 gms. cost 40 cts. I bought my figs, I washed them, and I ate them seated on the parapet of a square, on the town's outskirts. From there one could see Rome. The country-side gives one the impression of a sea. One always has the feeling that the sea is near.

Amuse yourself and dance well. I kiss you.

Thy Marguérite.

Marguérite's Journal—30th March, 1921—Frascati, near Rome

I imagined that it would be easy for me to find an hotel on arriving in Rome. As a matter of fact it was almost impossible at this time of year as Rome is full of tourists, and I had no choice but to decide to come to this small town not far away after having tried to get in at ever so many hotels in Rome.

Marguérite's Journal—4th April, 1921

I am afraid I am creating too much attention with my Paris hats and dresses and the bright plain skirt which I wear with my blazer. It is indeed difficult in a foreign country to go about alone. If I stop for more than a minute to look at a shop window, or even if I stop to look at something of archaeo-logical interest, I become an object of attention. Still, I have chosen to please myself and go where I wish so I am not going to let that worry me.

Having decided to come to Italy, P.L. has not yet found a room in any hotel in Rome. He has done what I was obliged to do and come to Frascati. I am rather glad. It will be a great help to me. This quiet place is just the place for a man like him still suffering the effects of the war. Besides, he will be spending less here than in London or France. 25 lire a day covers every-thing.

I shall have to be patient with him. I have to take him to Tusculum tomorrow. Apparently he spent part of his holiday with his mother and then joined one of his numerous girl-friends in Italy before he decided that he wanted to be on his own and went to Rome expecting to find me there, as he knew that I meant to go there before leaving Italy for France.

CHAPTER XIV

Husband and Lover

The letter in which she confesses that M. Legros has joined her is missing. From Frascati the post took between three to five days to reach London, and because Arnold's acknowledgement of the news is dated 4th April, one imagines that the missing letter was dated either 30th or 31st March. Meanwhile, on 3rd April, she was writing another long letter that made no mention of Legros. Significantly, it is endorsed 'A.B. 7.4.21', as receipt of all her letters in this series came to be endorsed, which may imply that he envisaged that someday their production might be required in a court of law.

Arnold Bennett Esq.,   Grand Hotel,
12B George Street,   Frascati,
London, W.1.   3rd April, 1921.

Mon grand chéri,
    It's Sunday. All the bells in Frascati are ringing out midday. It's the most delicious day since my leaving London because hitherto, both on the Riviera and here, the weather has been misty. I love Frascati more and more. I have completely given up the idea of staying in Rome. I shall remain here until I go to Toulouse. The Rome hotels are full. I went there yesterday and even with Cook's to help me I couldn't find anything. There were some very bad *pensions* where if I had to I could find a room, but I have a horror of *pensions*. More and more I like comfort. Here, although everything is very simple, I have it.
    In the hotel there are some French people, a German lady, and above all Italians. Altogether there aren't many people. I have a horror of talking with strangers; on the other hand, I often go into the shops and try to talk with the shopkeepers. It's marvellous how well I understand Italian, as, for example, to say 'bernique'.

Tell me if you have seen Olive. So Jean has left London! I scarcely hope to see him in Paris. The work goes all right, does it? And is the yacht bought yet? . . .

Mme. Arnold Bennett,   12B George Street,
Post Restante,   Hanover Square,
Roma.   London, W1.
                                                   4th April, 1921.

Mon enf. ch.,

At last I have a letter from you! And as so often, I am surrounded by mysteries! I don't think you and Legros understand how I look at the affair. You imagine that I take it much more seriously than I do. But I will enlighten you. What startles me, even to the point of making me laugh, is Legros' lack of *savoir vivre*. Legros can be a most charming man and a most agreeable companion, but his social clumsiness is astounding. And this is by no means the first instance of it. I have always treated Legros with the very greatest courtesy, and also with the very greatest hospitality (a hospitality, by the way, which he never attempts to return, apparently on the grounds of poverty, though he can find the money to wander up and down Italy with a lady!) Further, I have always treated him with the greatest intimacy and candour. Yet, though I see him constantly, he never says a word about going away for a holiday until the eve of his departure, when he comes in, without notice, and announces that he is going to Brittany to see his mother. Within about a week of this he is taking his mistress to meet my wife in an obscure town in central Italy; and I am supposed to believe that this meeting in Frascati, or Rome, or elsewhere, is a mere accident, arranged on the spur of the moment!! Let him exercise his imagination, if he has any, and conceive how he would have felt had he been in my place. He would assuredly have been intensely annoyed. And it was an immense social clumsiness on his part not to have foreseen that I should be annoyed. This social clumsiness is strange in a Frenchman, that mirror of good manners! I strongly resent his secrecy and want of *franchise*. I regard it as a very bad return for my constant good nature towards him. Even he must surely see that if I am to be treated in this way the relations between us cannot continue on the old footing. And it is absolutely certain that unless I receive some explanation and apology direct from him, our relations will *not* continue on the old footing. And you can tell him frankly that I say so. And what is more, if I do not hear from him, he will hear from me; he will receive a letter such as he will not soon forget. After all, some commonsense and some decency must be brought into this affair, and I shall bring them. Count on me, my child.

As for you, I think you might have telegraphed me of your change of place. Here am I writing day after day to San Remo —letters which you will almost certainly not get. To have telegraphed would have been easy, and I should not have been without news for five days. And I do wish you wouldn't keep on saying that you see so little of me. You know very well that you see far more of me than nine wives out of ten see of their husbands. As for Richard, my views remain the same. All I ask you to do is not to make yourself unpleasant and so to make my task even more difficult than it would be.

Your outburst at your last breakfast here was an inexcusable outrage.

We will now leave these matters.

I had neuralgia and dyspepsia for a week and couldn't do a stroke of work. It went off on Saturday. Yesterday I did a very good day's work, and today a fair day. I danced three times last week, and I shall dance three times this week. . . . The industrial situation in England is exceedingly grave, has never been so grave before. I don't know how it will end. But it will end somehow.

I have become rather friendly with Marjorie Gordon, a young musical comedy actress. But it is improbable that she will bring a young man with her to meet me in Timbuctoo by accident.

My poor child, I adore your hard bed and I kiss you well.

Nouche.

P.S. Let us hope that at the last moment poor Legros' mistress hasn't been prevented from going with him to Italy! You will be very kind if you will let me have a description of her when you see her. She intrigues me.

Arnold Bennett, Esq.,   Grand Hotel,
12B George Street,   Frascati,
Hanover Square,
London, W.1.   6th April, 1921.

Mon grand chéri,

. . . Yesterday, I made an excursion by car (naturally) to
Tusculum. I asked Pierrot to go with me. We didn't take a
guide, but we found a priest who explained all he knew about
the ruins of Cicero's villa which is in Tusculum. It's lamentable
to think that by pure bad luck such treasures are found in a
country that neither venerates nor exploits them.

All the ruins are very moving. Not far from Cicero's house
is a Roman theatre. It is small but admirably made and
preserved. I was not sure where the stage was. I deduced that
it was in front of the amphitheatre. I wanted to test the acoustics
myself. Admirable! I asked Pierrot to recite some lines. Then
in my turn I recited some passages from Molière's *Femmes
Savantes*. Unluckily some visitors interrupted my speech. I
didn't like to go on again for the same reason—visitors—
visitors—I would have loved to recite some passages from
Phèdre or *Andromache*.

I dismissed the car before we reached Frascati so that I could
walk across the fields and through the woods. Wild flowers were
everywhere, and there was a fine panorama. These hills of
Tusculum are quite beautiful. Near a monks' cloister stood a
Jesuit cloister. A peasant who met us told us that they (the
monks) spend their time doing penance for the Jesuit trials.

This hotel is filling up with travellers who can't find anywhere to stay in Rome. Some Germans and English have
arrived. Yesterday evening I had the wild idea of going to dine
at a village inn. What wonderful food, what wine! Afterwards
we went to a café where I had a fine Italian liqueur whose name
I forget.

My rheumatism is gone. I have a lovely complexion. I am a
little sun-burned. It suits me. I get up early. Today I shall go to
Rome to see the Forum. Your letters have come. What a
nuisance that you are suffering in the head so much that you
can't smoke! To think of it spoils my holiday. If I didn't know

that you were well cared for, reasonably happy, and surrounded by friends, I should catch the first train and soon be with you.

Now I must go. The train is due. I find it very agreeable to have a companion whom I can forget when I wish. You understand, don't you?

I kiss you, my great worker,

Thy wife, Marguérite.

Evidence of Arnold's uncertainty of mind when presented with the situation at Frascati rests in the existence, among the other letters, of a draft of the following. Amendments are far more numerous than was usual with him, and the finished letter much amplifies the draft. Again, how this draft could possibly have come into Marguérite's possession is a mystery.[1]

Mme. Arnold Bennett,	12ʙ George Street,
Poste Restante,	Hanover Square,
Roma.	London, W.1.
	6.4.21.

Mon enf. ch.,

Your second letter (i.e. her letter of the 1st April) from Frascati arrived today. It took 5 days to come. Your description of the town and district is very good, in your best style. As for me, my health is now very much better. Probably because of the dancing . . .

Although your letter is very interesting so far as it goes, it does not go very far. I notice that you give me no further information about how it has happened that Legros and his mistress are meeting you in Rome or in Frascati. The old policy of secrecy is apparently being followed. In my last letter I referred to Legros, but you know that you are more to blame about this affair. Supposing that *I* had been seeing Mary or Diana nearly every day for many months. Supposing that *you* had complained several times, not about the meetings, but about the fact that as a rule I did not tell you where I was. Supposing that *I* had insisted on having a free night a week, and that every such

---

[1] *A plausible explanation is that, before leaving Conmarques for the last time, she filched it and her own letters so as to remove evidence for divorce.*

night I spent with Mary or Diana. Supposing that *I* had demanded a long holiday alone, and that again and again I had insisted that I must be *alone* on my holiday. Supposing that on the night before my departure Mary or Diana had called and I had said to her, in front of you, having previously said nothing at all to you : 'I am expecting you to meet me in Italy,' and that afterwards I had still said not a word to you of my plans, though it was obvious that Mary or Diana and I had been discussing plans at length, and that I had gone off still without saying a word.

What would *you* have thought?

You would have thought either that I deliberately intended to annoy or insult you; or, alternatively, that I was a perfect fool. I should be a fool because I had not the imagination to foresee that you would be annoyed or hurt by my secretive conduct, or to foresee that you would be forced to write letters to me about it, which would interfere both with the pleasure of my holiday and the efficiency of your work while I was away.

Well, that is the case.

Mon enfant, you often call yourself a child and a fool. Your action proves that you are not far wrong in doing so. It is inevitable that I should treat you according to your action. I most certainly shall not tolerate such action. No husband who was not an idiot would tolerate it. Unless I receive not only full apologies from Legros, but also an expression of regret from you, my relations with Legros will be completely changed, and if you take any more holidays 'alone' you will pay for them yourself. No wife could be more free than you are. I give you far more freedom than I allow myself. But there is one freedom I will not give you, that is to say the freedom to behave improperly towards me. I don't object to your meeting anybody anywhere. You may be indiscreet—you are—but when I have warned you I say no more. What I object to is being kept in the dark and treated as if I did not exist.

Do not imagine that I am taking this affair tragically, nor that I have ceased to be absurdly fond of you. No ! The end of the world has not yet come. I merely mean that you have treated me with gross rudeness and total lack of consideration. You have acted as if I did not count. My intention is to show you that I do count. In the words of Molière, '*Tu l'as voulu, Georges Dandin*'.[1]

I forgot to tell you that the hospital is so busy that Fred [*his valet*] can't have his operation till the 14th and he will only have it then because he told the doctor that he was in the service of Arnold Bennett,

who kisses you well,

Nouche.

Arnold Bennett Esq.,   Grand Hotel,
12B, George Street,   Frascati,
Hanover Square,   nr. Rome, Italy.
London, W.1.   7th April, 1921.

Mon grand chéri,

It's dull and cold today . . . If only you knew how well I am! Frascati's good red wine is a laxative which does me good. I am so sun-burned that I shall find it impossible to appear décolletée in Paris and London. My journey from Rome to Toulouse will be so long that I shall perhaps be obliged to give it up. I don't know yet. In any case I still have a good week here, because I don't count on leaving before the 14th April. As I want to have a costume tailored in Paris I shall stay there for a week. At first I shall stay with the Bions. But you will have further news on the subject. I work. My poems are going all right. They are ready for when I get back. I have avoided writing letters. I don't know what Miss Rootham has done for our A.F.P.S. during her stay in Paris. As I hope to be back in London on the 26th or later, and as the first recital will not take place until the 5th May, I shall have time to prepare myself.

Yesterday, Legros and I went to Rome to see the ruins. The Rome streets are full of holes. I did a fine thing, I succeeded in spraining my right ankle. Happily Legros was with me. It happened on a tramline. You can imagine the pain it caused. Happily I didn't faint but I suffered a lot getting to the nearest

---

[1] 'You asked for it, Georges Dandin.' What Molière actually wrote was 'Vous l'avez voulu, Georges Dandin.'

chemist's. The chemist massaged the foot and bandaged it and declared that I could walk . . . and indeed I could walk. No need to tell you that I went by car the rest of the day! I left here at 9 a.m. and returned at 9.30 this evening. It's extraordinary how little tired I am. Truly, it is lucky that I am not alone. Just think how difficult it would be for me to find someone to go travelling with! Every one is either busy or likes to travel some other time. It happens that Legros and I understand each other perfectly, that he is useful to me and I am useful to him, that we are both French, that we understand things in the same way, and that two friends couldn't understand one another better. Should the question of 'sex' arise, it would destroy a wonderful friendship—it would be folly and bourgeois, and I am pretty certain that you aren't terrified by the idea that a man-friend is with me.

Are you better, my dear? I hope so. I no longer have a headache or a cough. Today you are at Brightlingsea with all the others. Has the *'Marie-Marguérite'*[2] been painted yet?

I kiss you,

Thy wife, Marguérite.

Postcard

Mme. Arnold Bennett,	12B, George Street,
Grand Hotel,	Hanover Square,
Frascati,	London, W.1.
nr. Rome, Italy.	8.4.21.

What a good prophet I am! I told you I thought L. would arrive alone. I am expecting letters from both of you, in the sense that I asked for.

N.

Extract from Marguérite's Journal—9th April, 1921

I went to Rome. Visited St. Peter's and the Vatican. I found at the Post Office a few letters and a postcard. A letter from Arnold. He is far from pleased to know that P.L. has joined me here.

[2] His new yacht.

Mme. Arnold Bennett,   12ʙ, George Street,
Grand Hotel,   Hanover Square,
Frascati,   London, W.1.
nr. Rome, Italy.   9.4.21.

Mon enf. ch.,

I have your letter in which you tell me about Legros coming alone, as of course I knew he would.

The whole letter shows that you felt you were doing something that you knew I should gravely disapprove of. And if you have acted for the best your best is very poor. All your reasons are perfectly absurd. But the worst thing is that you should have discussed your projects with various people, and said nothing whatever to me. The first and only thing I have heard of the matter was a question put to Legros in my presence. Not a word to me personally. If you have any commonsense at all you must realise that this sort of conduct must inevitably lead to trouble.

Either Legros is an absolute fool, or he has behaved scandalously.

I telegraphed you as follows this morning :

'I think you should ask Legros to leave immediately and cable me that he has left. Ton Arnold.'

I am now waiting to hear from both of you. I have shown the greatest patience in this affair. If I do not get satisfactory letters you may believe me that the trouble *will* be serious. Don't say afterwards that I haven't warned you.

Clark's first concert last night was a great success.

I kiss you, N.

Her reply was obviously written under great stress of emotion. One imagines that 'couche', interpreted as 'a hard bed', had some private significance. (For the original, see Appendix.)

Arnold Bennett Esq.,   Grand Hotel,
12ʙ, George Street,   Frascati,
Hanover Square,   nr. Rome, Italy.
London, W.1.   10th April, 1921.

Mon chéri,

More than ever it appears that I am a source of perpetual

torment to you . . . if it isn't Richard it's Legros . . . if it isn't Legros . . . it's allusions I make to the tangible or mysterious. It's not funny for a wife to feel for almost fourteen years that she is a naughty, capricious, and mysterious child; a being who must, from the very first day, totally yield herself and become merely a reflection of her husband. For ultimately that is the source of the vexations, torments, of which (you say) you are my victim! You do with me exactly as John Read does with his daughter Emilie, and I might reply to you as that young person (who had her own hard bed to lie on, too) replied to him : 'It isn't fair. One day you spoil me and the next I am wicked beyond belief ! . . . ' (or whatever she said).

So I shall spend my entire life making you suffer and begging your pardon! I must indeed be a child and have a hard bed to lie on !

As for Legros, perhaps I know him better¹ than you . . . but however hard my bed it doesn't stop me from knowing precisely where I stand regarding him. I have to thank you however for your solicitude in wishing to protect me from a young man whom you imagine is dangerous for a person of my years. It is not the case that, speaking generally, ordinary English wives see very little of their husbands, but that Legros helps me to resign myself to seeing very little of my own. Moreover, I don't suppose you place yourself in the category of ordinary men.

I have received all your letters and the others. Thanks. I have let Pierrot read your letter of the 4th April. He has written to you and, in his turn, has let me read his reply. I hope that all these complications and misunderstandings will now disappear. After all, life is short. Why don't we make it as easy as possible? If we don't succeed, who will? Don't forget that the friend I protect was a soldier who suffered six (sic) years of war, an unbalanced being whom friendship, encouragement, kindness, and help will bit by bit put back on his feet. It is my duty and pleasure to protect him, and I shall continue to do so, at least until he is back to normal. In occupying myself with him, I don't take anything away from you, I don't take anything away from anyone. That much you know as well as I.

In spite of a certain upset produced by your letters, I am happy and satisfied. My clearsightedness, my wisdom, and my philosophy, which you regard as a hard bed to lie on—these three things which make me so mysterious in your eyes, help me. I seem to be mysterious because you don't believe I possess them.

I beg you, be happy, don't torment yourself.

I learn with pleasure that you have made the acquaintance of a young musical comedy actress. These women who have charmed you and whom you charm are legion. I receive them as warmly as you receive the men-friends who admire me or to whom I like to render a service. All should be for the better; in my opinion all is for the better, my poor dear!

I have given up going to Toulouse, which would be too complicated a journey. These last few days it has been cold. I have got a twinge of rheumatism that I am nursing. Look after yourself, eat well, dance well. I have received your wire safely. Thanks.

I kiss you,
Your wife,
Marguérite.

Arnold Bennett Esq.,   Grand Hotel,
12B, George Street,   Frascati,
Hanover Square,   nr. Rome, Italy.
London, W.1.   [*undated*]

Mon chéri,

I shall leave Frascati on Thursday or Saturday to join the Rome-Paris express. Legros has been kind enough to go to Rome to buy my ticket. He has not yet come back. I foresee that the express will be booked up for Thursday. Consequently I shall very probably not be able to leave before Saturday. Since you always like to know everything in advance I tell you now. I will send you a telegram as soon as I arrive in Paris. I don't know yet if the Bions can have me. I am waiting to hear from them.

I am not so well today. I have a nervous headache, just like the ones I have so often in London. I have demonstrated to my own satisfaction that I shall never be able to escape this kind of misunderstanding, and if I upset you, you can boast of *always* doing the same for me.

I am not complaining, I am stating a fact.

I have had the misfortune again to sprain my foot. I take plenty of taxis . . . in any case, I could only go by taxi, with my London heels. Happily I have a pair of shoes for walking. The roads are vile – pointed cobbles . . . I have chafed the ankle, so I keep it bandaged. I am not infirm, nor outrageously lame, but the ankle is very weak . . . but these physical pains are nothing.

I envy these primitive simple-living people. I am spoilt by life . . . and until I die (which perhaps is not far off) luxury and comfort and clothes will doubtless be my vices. Can one ever escape one's vices when one is of mature age, or old?

Vanity, vanities . . . all is vanity . . .

To know it and to go forward . . . that's a mystery! . . . for you who are surrounded only by mysteries, as you so often say . . .

It is clear that men must console themselves with work, and women with resignation . . . when there is no harmony in their characters.

I embrace you,
Marguérite.

Mme. Arnold Bennett,   12B, George Street,
c/o Georges Bion,[3]   Hanover Square,
7, Rue José Maria de Hérédia,   London, W.1.
Paris VII.   13.4.21.

Mon enf. ch.,

Thank you for your dispatch received this morning. I do not understand why my telegram should take 4 days to reach you, and if you will keep it I will have enquiries made. Such delay is inexcusable. We now know how this affair stands, and although I do not mean to take it too seriously, I am bound to take notice of it. Having taken notice of it, I shall forget it.

[3] Marguérite's uncle by marriage.

You insisted to me many times that it was necessary for you to be absolutely alone on your holiday. You didn't want anybody at all.

But you were discussing plans for meeting Legros in Italy. Of this I knew nothing until the last moment, and then only the slightest hint of them by a question put by you to Legros, who answered in an evasive and self-conscious manner and immediately left the house.

There can be no doubt that the thing was deliberately concealed from me.

Before Legros joined you, you knew from my letters that I strongly objected to it. Nevertheless you did not stop him from joining you.

The excuses which you make in every letter are merely silly. You knew that you were doing something which I objected to, and which was wrong, and which you would condemn without pity in another woman.

All I have to say is that I have no intention of providing you with money to spend on continental holidays with Legros, my simple child, and that for one year from the present date I shall pay for no more holidays for you. So far as you are concerned I now forget the affair, though it has caused me a great deal of pain; and you may rely upon me not to let it influence my relations with my sweet child.

The case of Legros is different. Legros has behaved very rudely to me. With every intention of holidaying with my wife in Italy, he tells me that he is to stay with his mother and he tells me nothing else. I have always treated him, for your sake, with the greatest friendliness and intimacy. It was his business to talk to me of his plans, quite apart from anything that you might or might not have told me. To do so was the merest elementary politeness. Not to do so was proof of an intention to conceal. You and he may say what you like about his attitude to you, but the fact remains that he has left not only his mother but his mistress in order to be with you. I will not tolerate his behaviour to me. I absolutely refuse to do so. I insist that he shall write and apologise to me in the fullest possible manner. If he does so—and I quite expect that at a word from you he will—I shall forget what has passed and our relations will be exactly as before—for after all I am inclined to think that he has been merely silly and lacking in imagination, like you. If he does not, our relations will cease entirely, and when he comes into this house I shall go out. The matter will be solely in his hands.

If you think my attitude is wrong, find out what Georges Bion thinks; but tell him the whole of the facts. You are very friendly with him, you have confidence in him, and he adores you, and he is a member of your family. If he disagrees with my conduct in the affair I will make every apology. I want to be fair . . .

I kiss you well, my ingenuous wife,
Nouche.

Extract from Marguérite's Journal—13th April, 1921.
I have had a very serious stomach upset. I felt awful all night. Very likely it was due to my nervous system which had been rather upset by A.B.'s letters and his last wire. He is exaggerating a perfectly harmless situation. He is threatening me with all sorts of dire punishments. I am longing to get away from here to Paris.

Mme. Arnold Bennett,	12B George Street,
c/o Georges Bion,	Hanover Square,
7 Rue José Maria de Hérédia,	London, W.1.
Paris.	14th April, 1921.

Mon enf. ch.,

Thanks for your letter of the 10th which arrived at the same time as Legros'. I am glad to see that it contains no attempt to justfy that policy of secrecy towards me which cannot possibly be justified. It is this policy of secrecy of which I chiefly complain. I do not approve of certain things that you do in regard to Legros. I consider them highly indiscreet, to say no more; but, having warned you about them, and expressed my disapproval, I leave the matter at that. You are of course infatuated, quite innocently, with Legros. Such an infatuation might happen to anyone, and you cannot be blamed for it. The one thing for me to do is to treat it benevolently and understandingly and indulgently, and this I think I have always done. But I am bound to express my views, to do the little I can to influence you, and to take care that I myself am treated with consideration.

I cannot conceive any self-respecting husband doing less than I have done. Nor can I conceive any husband giving a wife more freedom, or being less exigent about her behaviour than I do and am. Nobody can say that I am difficult about your doings. You know this better than anybody.

My letter to you was not written for Legros to see, as you well know, and you were very wrong to show it to him.

As for your saying that I object to hearing of anything that is not positively decided—that is merely silly. You are perfectly well aware that all I object to is leaving *my own plans vague.* As an explanation of your policy of secrecy this is about the feeblest excuse you ever invented.

I have written to Legros. As he will only be at Florence for a few days my letter might miss him; so I enclose it with this for you to forward to him.

The matter is now ended.

It seems likely that the big strike will occur tomorrow. If it does, you will not be able to return till it is over. Fred has had his operation, and has come through it very well. He is now in bed.

I am going to a grand ball tonight with Olive.[4] This will be the last festivity before the strike.

I kiss you,
N.

Mme. Arnold Bennett,	The Reform Club,
c/o Georges Bion,	London, W.1.
Paris.	15th April, 1921.

Mon enf. ch.,

On leaving to go to the club to dine, I found your letter at the foot of the stairs, and I sat down to read it.

4 Olive Valentine, neé Ledward, whom the Bennetts had known at Fontainebleau.

Your letter is very sad. I expected it to be so. You deliberately do something to which you knew I should object, to which any husband would object, to which you would strongly object if I did it, and which you would mercilessly and sarcastically condemn in another woman, and when I effectively protest you say that men don't understand women and that death is near. Human nature, I suppose. I am very sorry about your sprained ankle. Give it repose. You have a terribly long journey in front of you, but I expect that as I write this it may be nearly over. I hope so.

I danced last night with Olive till 1.15. Fatigued, but brain clear. I dine at the club, tonight, tomorrow and Sunday! Fred is going on well. I return Kathleen's letter. I see nothing sad in it. On the contrary it is more cheerful than usual. But of course the world is a mass of gloom.

I kiss you, my poor one.

Nouche

Mme. Arnold Bennett,   12B George Street,
c/o Georges Bion,   Hanover Square,
7 Rue José Maria de Hérédia,   London, W.1.
Paris.   16th April, 1921.

Mon enfant chérie,

This afternoon while waiting for the Clarks, I received three letters from you; two of the 12th and one of the 13th. I enormously regret that you lost consciousness in the bathroom. But since at the same moment I received the new telegram of your arrival in Paris you must be much better. I don't find anything infantile in what I wrote. What displeased me, and what I will never support, is that the Italian project *à deux* was carefully concealed from me. No husband would support it tranquilly. And you know it. But I say no more. You write as though it were I who had been [illegible—?guilty of the impropriety]. Anyway . . .

On Monday I danced with the Clarks and a lady they brought with them. They stayed so late that I didn't have time to scribble this brief, hasty word, and to express my desire to see you. Alone, I am always very 'restless' and I continually search for distractions—feminine for the most part. I am engaged every evening of next week and on Sunday at the Phoenix theatre. Perhaps you will arrive on Monday, the 25th.

I kiss you well,
Nouche.

Arnold Bennett Esq.,   7 rue José Maria de Hérédia,
12B George Street,   Paris.
Hanover Square,
London, W.1.   20th April, 1921.

Mon chéri,

. . . In my opinion one can never do too much for war victims. I like to concentrate my efforts upon one of these victims and try to cure him by making him work—work which will bring him satisfaction and well-being so that ultimately he may marry —that is to say, to make a man of him. For after all, like so many others, Legros will finish by meeting a woman of his own age whom he will marry.

In Paris as in London one sees many neurasthenic men, tired of life by the war. I recognise them all and I feel sorry for them all. I would like to do the impossible and multiply to infinity all that I am doing for Legros. My only hope is that among them are some who have a woman friend, a wife, or a mistress, who understands them. I fear that yet again you find that hope infantile, and good enough for a woman with a hard bed to lie on . . . so much the worse. In the realm of feelings opinions differ. Feelings have no need to be organised; they operate at will in a limitless world in which they may be either appreciated or misunderstood, but in which their influence is considerable.

I hope you are better. I still have a weak right ankle. . . . I am a little unsettled . . . the kidneys. . . . I shall get back to normal bit by bit. Knowing that it's not fatal, I am not too uneasy!

[unsigned—endorsed 'A.B. 21.4.21']

Extract from Marguérite's Journal—27th April, 1921.

I came back home on Monday the 23rd. A.B. welcomed me at Victoria. I could recognise him a long way off. He was wearing

151

a new grey overcoat, a red carnation as usual in his buttonhole, and a silk handkerchief of the same colour could be seen in the pocket of his brown suit. Strange mixture of colours, yet it was attractive and gay.

No car or taxi waiting to take us home. No! He had hired a brougham—the same brougham he seems to love. There is a side to his character which I call ultra Victorian. His taking up dancing because he likes girls and because he must be up to date is in some ways a minor miracle.

So Arnold forgave her. Not only that but he invited Legros to continue to visit them.

Marguérite's Journal—4th May, 1921

P.L. telephoned to ask me to let A.B. know that the person whom he had invited to an evening with the 'maître' and Mrs. Bennett would not be free. 'Please ask which evening would suit A.B. best.' P. seems to be surrounded with friends. I advised him to read a book on autosuggestion by Coué; he is so much better, almost a new man. My influence on him started on the 22nd January, 1920, the first time he called. He sat on a sofa not far from my armchair, and I can still hear him say, 'Madame, as far as I am concerned, life is over.' I learned from his friend Robert Nichols that he had been in the French army throughout the war.

Marguérite's Journal—7th May, 1921

It was no easy matter persuading Arnold to join me in a short visit to our country home. He left the place on the 30th September last and since then has not once wanted to come back. The house is well looked after and is always ready for us at any time. I love Comarques. Brightlingsea is not far away and A.B. can go to see his yacht there. He spoke of leaving me alone at Comarques the very moment we arrived. This rather annoyed me as at first he had said he was to stay with me here for a week. He is going to his yacht on Monday and means to stay on board until Wednesday of the following week. He has, however, asked me to join him and to bring P.L. with me.

Marguérite's Journal—5th June, 1921

I called at Thackeray Mansions before lunch. Annie opened the door and said, 'Mr. Bennett is here.' I immediately thought that he had wanted to talk to P.L. privately. They were in the dining-room and the door was closed. When they entered the sitting-room both men were very taken aback. My husband said: 'Strange, I must have only just arrived here when you came.' Whatever reason A.B. had for calling on P.L., I was quite happy that he had. Apparently he told him that he approved of our friendship and that it was a very good thing for me. It is an excellent thing to clear one's conscience when one knows that one is in the wrong, and A.B.'s conscience must have been pricking him. That visit has certainly bound us closer together. Arnold left before I did and said very nicely to us, 'Have a good time, you two.' He went straight to George Street in order to get on with his novel, while P. and I went for our usual Sunday walk in Hyde Park.

It is difficult not to understand the next series of letters as a massive and continuous effort on Arnold's part to hold together a crumbling marriage.

Mme. Arnold Bennett,
[*Apparently delivered to Comarques by hand.*]

Yacht *Marie-Marguérite*,
Bembridge,
Isle of Wight.
20.6.21.

Mon enf.,

I shall now speak plainly. If your behaviour to me does not fundamentally alter, my behaviour to you will fundamentally alter. I should have thought that the inexcusable Italian episode which you never even attempted to defend, because you could not, would have taught you a lesson. But it seems not. You have been worse than ever. You said to me that I was always secretly working against you, that I had you fast in a cage, that I was determined you should fail in everything. It was the contrary of the truth. There was absolutely no excuse for it. Two days later, when you were obliged to realise the monstrous injustice of your accusations, you tried to justify yourself by saying that

154

I had written you a letter in which I had said that I intended to break the friendship between you and Legros. This again was the contrary of the truth. If I wanted to separate you and Legros I should simply breathe one word to the University Authorities that I objected to his attitude towards you, and Legros, professor to young ladies, would be asked to resign, and he would never get another situation in England because he would not get a certificate of character from Bedford College. And that would be the end of Legros in England. Happily I am all in favour of the friendship between you and Legros, provided the conventions are strictly observed.

Not satisfied with your previous accusations you said a few days later that you suspected me of regularly committing adultery at a certain period of the war. Even if you have such disgusting suspicions you should not speak them without some cause.

Further, you are constantly saying to others in my presence that you never see me, and that the only opportunity you have of discussing private domestic matters with me is in the presence of strangers. This has become one of your cliché phrases. It is absolutely untrue. You see much more of me than most wives see of their husbands, and you have ample opportunity of discussing everything with me. If you do not see more of me the fault is your own. Who insisted, violently, on having a month's absence from me three times a year and one night every week, because she saw too much of me and needed relief from my 'powerful personality?' Was it you, or am I dreaming?

Further, I maintain that you deliberately neglect me; and yet I should have thought that my friendly attitude towards your relations with Legros (which no French husband and jolly few English husbands would permit) would have caused you to take special care not to neglect me. But no! I am left day after day to have tea alone. I am only working, it seems, so I do not matter. You go out for the whole afternoon, sometimes for the whole day; you return in time for dinner. You say not a word as to where you have been. Once when I told you that you might at least be in sometimes for tea, you replied ferociously: 'I am not a slave,' and when I said that you might be polite you replied: 'Polite? You are my husband.'

155

Marriage is a *mutual* contract, and the wife's part is a great deal more than mere housekeeping. The wife, who has no financial responsibilities, should supply agreeableness and attention and charm. You will say that it is sometimes difficult to do so. Of course it is. The worst *Mégère* (shrew) on earth can be charming and attentive when everything goes smoothly.

For a husband, where is the point of being married to a wife who is always unjustly accusing him and who neglects him? She keeps house for him, but he could get forty housekeepers.

You will always grumble; you will always pose as a martyr; you cannot help that; you are of a melancholy, suspicious, and jealous disposition, and I am very sorry for you, and quite prepared to accept the natural consequences of it. But the other things I will not stand. They are quite different, they must be altered, or my whole attitude to you will be altered. No one can be more charming, agreeable, and attentive than you, if you choose. You had better think about it. All the generosity is not going to be on one side. If you cannot behave to me as I behave to you there will be a notable change, my child. Why should I keep both your father and your mother, except for the reason that it pleases me to be agreeable to you? Why should I give you the very large allowance of £700 a year (—I should like to know another author's wife who gets as much!—) except for the reason that I like to please you. There is no other reason why I should give you any regular allowance at all. There is no other reason why I should help you in your Poetry Society. There is no other reason why I should tolerate your very close friendship with Legros.

I could give other examples, but perhaps I have given enough.

I have no greater pleasure than to give you pleasure, but unless your behaviour completely alters, that pleasure will cease. Is this plain? It is impossible to argue with you, because you at once make a scene, call me bad names, and then express surprise that I cannot '*discuter en ami!*' . . . I have had more than enough of arguments. All I want is a complete change. I have feared for years that I should have to write this letter. You now have it.

If you decide to keep me as a friend you have only to write

me that you will join me on the yacht in September. I shall be delighted.

Don't answer this letter impulsively.

Much depends on your answer,

Your still loving husband,

A.B.

Marguérite replied to the foregoing on the 21st June but her letter, which is so charged with emotion that it is barely intelligible, was never sent. It contains the following passage.

. . . He wants her (his wife) to arrive on board his yacht smiling, and from that moment always to be at his disposal when he needs her smile for the few moments he can spare, between a couple of paragraphs. One day he will tell her, 'I want to be left alone,' and the next day, 'I have people to tea,' and the day after that, 'You have people to tea, but I want mine here, in my study,' and the following day, 'I shan't be coming back till 6 o'clock;' when in London he works all week, Saturdays, Sundays, and holidays, and he goes to his club for amusement because at home he only has his wife.

The note she actually sent back is lost but Arnold's reply conveys his satisfaction.

Mme. Arnold Bennett,   *Yacth Marie-Marguérite,*

12B, George Street,   Southampton.

Hanover Square,

London, W.1.   23rd June, 1921.

Mon enf.,

I have your letter this afternoon. I hope you perceive now, how accusations affect others! You talk of a separation, as you always do when you are criticised. Believe me, I have no desire whatever for a separation. Neither have you any desire for a separation. It seems to me that you want to be free always to criticise me, but if I criticise you, you instantly talk of a separation! This is merely absurd . . .

Mme. Arnold Bennett,   Yacht *Marie-Marguérite*,
12B, George Street,   Southampton.
Hanover Square,
London, W.1.   (Next address: Dartmouth.)
                                                            24th June, 1921

Mon enf. ch.,

I have received your second letter with pleasure. I am very glad indeed that young Wolfe[1] is going to Comarques with Legros, and that he is going to paint your portrait. This portrait will be very interesting. We leave here tomorrow morning. As I had asked Dr. Keeble and Lillah [McCarthy, i.e. Lady Keeble] to spend a week on the yacht, I have written him asking them to come for Cowes week which begins on August 1st. I could do with another woman to complete the party and partner Lillah, and I should ask Miss Gordon except for the difficulty about the cabin. The small cabin is not suitable for a woman, and especially for an actress!

Extract from Marguérite's Journal—2nd July, 1921

At last I am out of London. I have been extremely busy these last few days. The flat, (12B, George Street) had to be seen to as we shall not be using it for the whole summer . . . Our guests, Edward Wolfe and P., (whom I call Pierrot) came by the same train. Teddy, that is Edward Wolfe, talked a great deal. He is very pleasant and extremely kind. He is about 25 years old and of medium height with remarkably fine cut features . . . Not long ago he completed a fine picture of my husband, and he has come here to paint my portrait.

---

[1] Edward Wolfe, the painter

Mme. Arnold Bennett,   Yacht *Marie-Marguérite*,
Comarques,
Thorpe-le-Soken.   5th July, 1921.

Mon enf. ch.,

Here we are at sea on our way to Plymouth. Still superb
weather—too superb. Calm sea. I have had a chill but am quite
better now. I have almost finished my novel. I long to reinte-
grate the conjugal bed. Every evening I nearly always dream,
and in these dreams the *enf. ch.* does everything I ask of her,
and above all when she knows that I am waiting . . . Eventually
follies and stupidities result. At times it's tiring.

> I kiss you well,
> Nouche.

Marguérite's Journal—22nd July, 1921

Arnold has just left. During the few days he was here he was
far from pleasant to all of us—and was especially unpleasant
to me. There was no question of my kissing him goodbye. One
dared not ask him for anything. Fred Harvey (the valet) took
him in the old Ford with a lot of provisions for the yacht packed
in it . . . champagne, cigars, cigarettes, a gramophone, and
records. Arnold did not say goodbye to me and he was far from
courteous to our guests . . . Not long ago he said to me, out of
the blue, 'I am not a machine for making money.'

Mme. Arnold Bennett,   Yacht *Marie-Marguérite*,
Comarques,   Southampton.
Thorpe-le-Soken.   23.7.21.

My child,

. . . On the first four nights of my short stay, Friday, Saturday,
Sunday and Monday, you chose to spend the evening with
Legros instead of with me. It is true that on the first night I was
asked if I would go for a walk. I said I preferred not to, and
you left me. On the other three nights you completely ignored
me, asked me nothing; walked straight out, took Legros away
from me, and disappeared for two hours with him and Miss
Lermite.[2] On the fourth night, Monday, you returned through
the garden arm in arm with Legros, Miss Shermitte walking

discreetly a few places in front. You were utterly absorbed in each other, so much so that you did not even see Wolfe and myself sitting close by as you passed. Legros enters the house and without hesitation shuts the door. Bang goes the door : Krrk goes the key in the lock! And I have to knock for admittance. 'I thought you were in,' says Legros. Not the fact. He didn't think, nor ask, nor look, though I was approaching the door as he banged it. With one of his grand, possessive gestures he acted by instinct, absorbed, and banged the door. Of course he didn't do it on purpose. He would have cut his hand off sooner than do it. But what a symbolic act! And it could never have occurred had you not been so infatuated that you didn't dream you were grossly neglecting me.

Rather alarmed by my demeanour after this, you were most attentive the next morning, most charming. Would I go and bathe? If not, would I like you to stay at home with you? Things are improving, I thought. I thought I should have the pleasure of your society in the evening. I was mistaken. You said : 'I am going to be by myself.' And you walked about the garden by yourself, no doubt doing urgent work.

On Wednesday night, after my visit to London, you asked me into your boudoir, and we did get some chat—until Legros, wondering what on earth husband and wife could be doing, came and disturbed us.

On Thursday afternoon I had to work and was therefore unworthy of attention. When you told Legros you would take him to bathe he did suggest that you might stay for tea. But no! You said sharply : 'Do you want to bathe or not, Pierrot?' Pierrot said that he did. 'Well then, we shall go at once. Arnold can have his tea with Wolfe.'

The tea would not have delayed you 15 minutes. You had 3 hours. But no! You could not wait. You must get away with Legros. After 3 hours of Legros you return to dinner, a little late. At 7.45 you go out again. I am talking to Legros in the garden. You take him off. You and he take a few hesitating turns at the pond, and then you disappear, infatuated. So infatuated that you see nothing extraordinary in the proceeding. I wait three quarters of an hour. I then go in. This is my last

² *A friend of Wolfe's.*

night. Astounded that I am hurt, you actually try to discuss the matter, before everyone!

Legros absolutely absorbs you. Even at the table in front of everybody you cannot help telling him that you 'almost love' him. Of course everybody notices your infatuation, and there must be a good deal of talk about it. But you don't see it. You don't even see, except by short glimpses, soon past, that you grossly neglect me in favour of Legros.

But *you* cannot see it. You think I am mad. You say it is all perfectly innocent. I know it is all perfectly innocent. But it is amazingly stupid, amazingly indiscreet, amazingly rude to me, and amazingly ridiculous. Neither you nor Legros seem to have any *savoir vivre*. Even for your own sakes it would have been advantageous to be polite and attentive to the old gentleman during his short stay.

Nor have you the sense to take the warnings which I have already given you.

The next time I have any complaint to make, I shall proceed to action. I shall deal direct with Legros, and also I shall put the whole matter before Georges Bion, in the hope that he may advise you. You need advice. And you have no one here except Legros, who is extraordinarily stupid in important things. Legros of course, though amiable enough, is only what the English call your 'tame cat'.

You understand : I shall not warn you any more. You see Legros almost daily in London during most of the year; you spend most of the summer with him at Thorpe. If you insist also on meeting him on the Continent there will be trouble. This is positive. If you cannot control your infatuation, I must help you to control it. Please don't waste time in saying that all you did at Comarques this week was for my benefit; that I understand nothing; or that you will commit suicide; or that I ought to separate from you. You won't commit suicide and I have not the least intention of separating from you. Why? Because I am fond of you.

I hope you will not compel me to prove that I am master of the situation in any unpleasant way. I much prefer to prove it pleasantly.

I kiss you,
A.B.

Extracts from Marguérite's Journal—27th July, 1921

For the last 24 hours I have been out of my mind. It was caused by a terrible letter from my husband. He accuses me of all sorts of crimes . . . indeed he has gone too far this time. There is nothing for it but to see my solicitor . . . I think the best thing I can do is not to answer the letter. If I do answer it, I am beaten before I start. The greatest of all crimes of which he accuses me is what he calls my 'lack of self-control' . . . I am completely at his mercy. It is quite probable that he is only too eager that I should continue being what I still am for him—a nurse (unpaid), an interesting and capable hostess, a fairly economical wife, a woman who knows how to dress well, and who is popular with his friends, male and female. In two words he still needs me.

She acknowledged his letter with a short note expressing the hope that the two young actresses he was expecting on board would keep him amused, and on 1st August wrote to him more fully. This letter, written in garbled English, betrays her state of mind by its incoherence. 'I am so glad that you don't have a wife on board who takes notes and when she is gone writes you long threatening letters—you have all the rights over me of an Englishman over his wife but you have many reasons for being nice to me, for how could I go on accepting your abnormal sexual habits—' Much is illegible.

Mme. Arnold Bennett,   Yacht *Marie-Marguérite.*
Comarques,
Thorpe-le-Soken.   4th August, 1921.

My child,
    Thanks for your letter of the 1st received yesterday afternoon. I am very glad that you have not attempted any answer to the complaints which I made; because there was none. In reply, you merely make complaints against me, which is natural. However, if my behaviour can be changed to suit you, I am only too willing to change it. I have not asked you to 'court' me. I hate being courted by women, and I know something about that!

All I asked was that you should not neglect me. As regards courting you, I assume that you do not expect me to compete with Legros for your society! It is a striking example of your methods to refer to my sexual habits. You always expect that you should be judged by a different standard from anybody else. What about *your* sexual habits? You didn't learn anything from me. In the same way you constantly accuse me of egotism. It doesn't occur to you that your own egotism is intense. Only your intense egotism prevented you from foreseeing that the way you have treated me, in connection with Legros, was absolutely certain to exasperate me in a high degree. When you accuse me of egotism I laugh. When I accuse you of egotism your face is covered with an ugly scowl and you are furious.

All these are details. The point is that I have always treated you with both material and moral generosity. And particularly so in regard to your friendship with Legros. If this generosity is to continue I am determined that you shall treat me with the greatest consideration and attention. I should have thought that the least you could do, in return for my benevolent attitude towards the Legros affair—an attitude of which not one husband in a thousand would be capable—would be to take particular care that I should not suffer. You yourself would never treat me with similar generosity in similar circumstances. You couldn't do it. Also I am determined that your arrangements with Legros shall not be hidden from me until they are definitely decided. I will not always be confronted with the *fait accompli*. And also I absolutely decline to agree to your spending holidays with Legros on the continent. You see quite enough of him in England. You may think that I am insisting too much : but I am anxious that there should be no possibility of misunderstanding on these points between us. It is very little that I am asking—and it is much less than most husbands would demand and enforce—but what I am asking I am asking, and if you cannot or will not agree to it then I shall have no alternative but to change my attitude fundamentally. You know that I am very fond of you—nothing but my fondness for you has led me to treat you as benevolently as I have—and I am exceedingly anxious that everything should go smoothly and that you should be as happy as I can make you. I have no fear

163

of losing your respect—not the slightest. Or my own self-respect.

You will receive all the money you need in ample time, whether I am in Brittany or not.

I kiss you,

N.

Marguérite's Journal—5th August, 1921.

A.B.'s letter put me quite out of my wits. I wish I had not read it. I can't understand what he is driving at. It sounds as if he is very attached to me while at the same time he is absolutely tired of me. What will come of all this?

Her reply is lost. Arnold's further letter of the 5th, from Cowes, includes the following passages:

My wife,

As you object to the word 'child' I will no longer use it.

Naturally I expect you to keep our house as my wife. I am very fond of you, and I know that you are very fond of me, and my one desire is that everything should go smoothly. Anything that I can do I shall be very willing to do. But anyone would think from your letters that in protesting again and again against your continued unsatisfactory treatment of me, I had committed some crime and that I was to blame, while you were a victim!

This is not so. That I have had just cause for complaint is unquestionable. I am bound to complain; I am bound to protest and to point out that if proper treatment is refused on one side it will be refused on the other. The matter depends entirely on your good sense, and as I have confidence in your good sense I hope it will end happily.

Extracts from Marguérite's Journal—10th August 1921.

I had a nervous breakdown on Sunday night. I was very sick from 2 o'clock in the night, and had fits of sobbing and talking

164

aloud. Stannard, the housekeeper, was very good to me. She told me that at the time she thought I was going mad and spoke of sending for the old doctor. I would not let her as I knew that I would have talked and probably said that I hated A.B. . . . that I could not stand the sight of him any more, that he ought to be told I was ill but that if he came near me I would kill him.

However, another factor in the form of two visitors was about to affect the marriage. These were her aunt and uncle, Hélène and Georges Bion, whom Marguérite described thus: 'I am six years younger than she. She fusses too much about everything and everybody. Her husband is very different. He is well brought up, cultured, honest, and kind-minded. You can never tell with my aunt. She is a born intriguer.' Arnold himself much respected Georges Bion. Before her marriage, it will be remembered, Marguérite had joined with Hélène in a gown-shop, which failed. Hélène was not only a kinswoman, she was a Frenchwoman deeply interested in subtleties of relationship and behaviour—and she was to arrive at Comarques when Marguérite was in despair.

Marguérite's Journal—22nd August, 1921

This morning the house was turned upside down. P.L.'s room is needed for M. and Mme. Bion, who are due to arrive from Paris tomorrow. I helped with the work and everything is in order again. I decorated the rooms myself and we now have flowers everywhere. I still can't read or write. I seldom think about my coming journey to Ostende. Shall I have the courage to go? I had a very non-committal letter from my husband. Apparently I addressed him a postcard without having written anything on it. I still fear his letters.

24th August, 1921

A.B. is not coming. I am rather glad. He is sailing on to Cornwall and from there will go to Ostende.

Hélène Bion, the mother of my two cousins, came into my boudoir about ten last night and stayed talking until midnight.

This talk was crucial, not because of what Marguérite told Hélène but because of what one imagines Hélène later told her husband:

Just as I guessed. When I say 'guessed' I really mean *knew*. She showed me some of his letters. My dear, she's kept every once since before they were married! Some of them are absolutely atrocious. I don't say she's exactly free from blame. You remember, Georges, how headstrong she always was. And of course she's infatuated with that clever young man. But it's deeper than that—much deeper. Arnold treats her as though she were a mistress. He *uses* her. Love? My dear, if that's love —if he *ever* loved her—it's the love of a camel. Seven years ago he was sending her a four-page letter from his first yacht —you remember the *Velsa*?—ticking her off because she'd taken a poster from his study. The other day it was six pages on the subject of Legros. He writes as though she were ten years old or a near-imbecile. My dear, the man's not *sane* : instead of writing to her about Legros why doesn't he show him the door and take his proper place here as her husband? Sailing up and down the Channel with a gramophone and a couple of actresses—! Of course, Marguérite's distraught!

Such would have been her drift, while Georges would have asked : 'Where does she stand at law? Does she own anything except her clothes?'

And Mme. Bion would have answered : 'Speak to her, Georges. But remember—beneath it all, she still adores Arnold.'

Marguérite's Journal—11th September, 1921

V. arrived from London to join me to go to Ostende where Arnold is expecting us both in his yacht. She is very reserved and the Bions are puzzled by her. She is a tall and lovely woman eager to please Arnold and myself. For myself, I would have preferred to go to Ostende alone, but Arnold insisted that V. should join me.

The V. mentioned was Olive Valentine, a war-widow in her early twenties and one of those pretty women with whom Arnold liked to surround himself. As a girl of sixteen she had stayed with the Bennetts at Fontainebleau—was in fact of a Burslem family, the

Ledwards, of whom the most distinguished was her brother Gilbert, the sculpter. Today, after reading the present book in typescript, she says : 'I had no idea how deeply he loved her. What I remember of Zeebrugge is how unhappy they both were. In particular Marguérite's wretchedness is something I cannot forget.'

Marguérite's Journal—15th September, 1921

Zeebrugge, on the Yacht *Marie-Marguérite*. The Bions are alone at Comarques in the care of the servants—they will return to France in a few days. The *Marie-Marguérite* was at her moorings but it was 8.45 before we found her.

Marguérite's Journal—16th September, 1921

Today is my birthday. On my dressing-table I found flowers from V. and a present from Arnold : an old shawl and a small cheque. He came into my cabin and wished me many happy returns of the day.

During the night I had made up my mind to keep my word to my Uncle Georges Bion about A.B. securing my future. I had to admit to my Uncle that up to now, after fourteen years of married life, Arnold had done nothing whatever to ensure my future security. My uncle had had no idea that such a situation existed. His enquiry was prompted by his amazement at seeing such a wonderful establishment at Comarques and the luxurious life we were living, with an immense staff of servants, a secretary, and a yacht. He said among other things that the last time he had seen Arnold in Paris he had looked very tired, that A.B. was at a dangerous time of life, and that it was time for me to think about myself and my future security. Uncle Georges Bion asked me a few questions after pointing out that judging by my ways, manners, and dress, I was a rich, spoilt woman, whereas in fact I owned nothing. First question : is Comarques your own? No. Second question : is the farm (adjoining Comarques) yours? No. Third question : what about the yacht? Of course not. Everything belongs to Arnold. Fourth question : Has he taken out an insurance policy on your life? No. My uncle was amazed and thought we were mad to live so dangerously.

I must admit that I had never thought of asking my husband to give me Comarques or anything else beyond the allowance for my dresses and pocket-money—and of course for housekeeping. My uncle was well aware that I would see Arnold at Ostende, and he made me promise that I would ask him for Comarques.

My chance of speaking to him had come. I took my courage in both hands and said : 'Thank you for your present. I would rather like something else from you.' 'What is it?' 'I want you to give me Comarques.' 'Never!' I was courageous enough to say, 'My dear, please think the matter over, and when you come back to London and the flat we might talk the matter over seriously.' My husband left the cabin without a word.

Perhaps Arnold had, nevertheless, taken the hint that his wife possessed nothing of her own, because at breakfast next morning she found a cheque for £25 from him on her plate. Not only that, but in Ostende the same day he bought her a ring for 25,000 frs. and suggested that she invite the Bions to stay on board for a few days.

They arrived on the 22nd.

Marguérite's Journal—23rd September, 1921

My aunt thinks that A.B. is too attentive to V. I tried to explain that she is a member of the family, and that she is a nice woman whom I trust. The answer was that I was blind. She suggested that we should leave them for a day and take a train for Bruges.

At Bruges we visited the shops. We went into a jeweller's where we were shown an antique piece of local jewellery. I enjoyed buying a souvenir for Mme. Bion and bought her some lovely diamond earrings. They are rather showy but they suit her. For myself I bought a ring of gold with an emerald set in it. We returned to Ostende by the late train and found V. and Arnold at the station waiting for us. They also had had a nice day by themselves as M. Bion and the boys had spent the day visiting Ostende. So everything went well.

24th September, 1921

The Bions left us today for Paris. I am anxious to get back to

London to get the flat ready for the winter. Arnold will follow later. V. and I are leaving Ostende tomorrow. Arnold will see us off.

2nd October, 1921

George Street. I have enjoyed these first few days immensely. Complete freedom. Nobody to find fault with the meals served a few minutes late or early . . . no remarks about the dust on the furniture or things not quite in their correct place . . . no effort to hide physical or mental suffering . . . no effort to produce a smile to order. Wonderful.

Everything in the flat was just so when Arnold came back. I was tyrannised by the thought of having to talk to him about Comarques. When he has once said no or yes nothing can make him change his mind. Consequently I think I shall have to let the matter drop. I shall however ask him to raise my annual allowance from £750 to £1,500 and tell him that I would pay £60 for a life insurance and charities, and invest most of it.

She brought herself to make the demand with the result that the following letter was placed on her dressing-table. On the envelope, in French, in Arnold's handwriting, are the words: 'Don't tear this letter up without reading it. It is serious. I shall come back at 7 o'clock. I can't stay to tea.'

Marguérite.
By hand.

12B, George Street,
Hanover Square,
London, W.1.
1.10.21.

You have put me in a very difficult situation, and I don't know what to do. But there is one thing that is quite clear, and I have no hesitation as to it whatever.

You make a certain demand from me.

In reply I say: 'If I consent, either I shall have to sell the yacht, or we cannot continue to live in two houses.'

These are the exact words I used.

Immediately you make a scene. You say that I intend to sell Comarques.

You call me *Crapule* [blackguard], *crapule, crapule.*

You say further that unless I agree to your demand without any conditions you will 'lead me a dog's life', etc., etc.

I have no hesitation whatever in telling you clearly that unless you offer me your excuses for this scene, I shall have no further negotiations with you. My only reply to such conduct will be and must be : *'Fais.'*

If you apologise we can continue. If you feel that this is impossible I shall quite understand.

A.B.

Even then, the marriage hung on. To please her, Arnold went so far as to invite Legros to dinner. They went to the theatre together and attended a dinner at the H. G. Wells's. But the question of a settlement on Marguérite remained.

Marguérite's Journal—8th October, 1921

Instead of telling me what he had decided about securing my future, A.B. just put a note on my dressing-table. To avoid risking an upset I refused to read it and gave it back to him. He said, 'Very well, everything is finished between us.' 'As you wish,' I said, 'but tell me what you wanted me to do in your letter and I will do it. Why write?'

Arnold.   12B, George Street,
By hand.   Hanover Square,
                                                                London, W.1.

Mon cher Arnold,

I don't want to see the offer you have made me. Over 14 years I have given you the best in me, my youth, my energy, my love. I believe I have done for you everything that a woman humanly can do for her husband—now that you are rich and famous you have no more need of me.

171

Perhaps it would be better if we were to separate. I will think about the advice you gave me to go and see my solicitor.

Marguérite.

Marguérite.
By hand.

12B, George Street,
Hanover Square,
London, W.1.
9.10.21.

Dear Marguérite,

Please do not twist my words. What I said was that if you refused to read my statement everything was finished between us as regards this affair. *Under no circumstances shall I give way about this.* But I certainly should not be so ridiculous as to suggest a separation because you refuse to read my statement.

You frequently, however, talk of a separation. You seem really to want it. If so you must go to your solicitor, who will communicate with me. Separations are complex legal things. I think I should be acting unfairly in continuing to object to a separation if you want it.

The statement which you refuse to read contains a very handsome offer, but it is not an acceptance of your demand. I assume therefore that I must not give it to you a third time. If you decide to read it you will find it in the middle drawer of my desk.

I shall not be in for lunch. This afternoon I go to the Sharpes. I shall be in for dinner tonight.

Yours, A.B.

Attached to the above was a note reading: 'I have written a statement of our financial situation for you, and made you a very handsome offer. You refuse even to read it. Very well. If you change your mind, let me know. A.B.'

Yet on the 19th they entertained three guests to dinner, including Legros, before the party set out 'in the old brougham Arnold had ordered' for Lady Swindling's where Marguérite gave a recital of French poetry . . . Sensitive as she was, boasting an artistic temperament, and given to headaches, she could neverthe-

172

less learn ten poems by heart and deliver them to a distinguished gathering of which her husband was one. He, too, the most intuitive writer of his day, could sit through it, watch her, and listen to her.

Next morning, having taken a sleeping draught, she was obliged to get up to answer the phone : the call was from Arnold's solicitor, Braby. She saw him at 3 p.m. 'Really, Arnold is mad. For nearly two years he had been only too glad that I had such a friend in P.L., and now he is insisting that I drop my protégé entirely.' She saw this as a move in the arranging of a settlement on her, and it is to her credit that she absolutely refused. But the ultimatum had been made, give up Legros or we separate, and Arnold was the last man to go back on his word.

Marguérite's Journal—21st October, 1921

I had breakfast in the dining-room as usual. A.B. did not expect to see me there. He said nothing—as usual—and read his papers. It had been decided that we should both go to a concert at Cedric Sharpe's, the 'cellist's. I asked Arnold at what time it was to begin. His answer was, 'With whom are you going?' I answered, 'With you, of course.' He retorted, 'Nothing of the kind. If you are going, I won't.' He gave me the tickets and I took only one. As he left the room I asked him if he would be in to dinner. He said, 'I shall take no more meals in this house.'

There is no evidence that they ever met again. She went to the concert alone and there met Braby, who verbally told her the terms, not of a settlement, but of a separation. A letter confirming them arrived by first post next day; one of the conditions was that she should leave the George Street flat at once.

That night she slept at the Empress Club.

The terms of the settlement were in the last degree generous.

Arnold Bennett Esq.,   Addressed as from
12B, George Street,   12B George Street,
Hanover Square,   but written from the
London, W.1.   Empress Club, Dover Street,
                                             London, W.1.
                                        25th October, 1921.

Mon cher Arnold,
    I have the impression that Braby only helps to muddle things.
    In growing older I become more and more French while
you become more and more English. You will be more at peace
without me and I shall be more at peace without you.
    All I want is my liberty and something to live on. £2,000 a
year until I die and a sum of £5,000. You know very well that
with the habits to which you have accustomed me I could not
live with less.
    Nothing could be simpler than for us to do as we did during
the war: you shall have your home and I mine. We could
see each other from time to time and I should certainly come
to nurse you if you needed me.
    If you prefer me to live abroad, I am ready to do so.
              With my affectionate sympathy,
                  Marguérite.

Mme. Arnold Bennett,   12B, George Street,
c/o Empress Club,   Hanover Square,
35, Dover Street,   London, W.1.
London, W.1.   25.10.21.

My dear Marguérite,
    I appreciate the friendly tone of your letter.
    I do not think that Braby has made any confusion. My offer,

which you first accepted and then declined, is perfectly clear :
£2,000 a year provided that it is not more than one quarter
of my net income.

If in any year the sum paid to you should be less than £2,000,
and if in a subsequent year my net income should exceed
£8,000, then the balance not previously received by you to be
made up accordingly.

£5,000 capital at my death, if I die before you, and the
income for your life of two thirds of my estate after this £5,000
has been paid.

If you accept this offer please tell Braby at once. He must
deal with the matter, not I.

If you decline it, it will be withdrawn entirely and you must
take your own course.

I wish you to understand that I cannot possibly undertake
to pay you £2,000 a year whether my income falls or not.

I think it would be an excellent thing for you to go and live
on the continent. Let me advise you that what you want more
than anything else is repose.

It would be very unwise for you and me to meet at present.

I am full of sympathy for you : so is everybody.

Yours, A.B.

He was equally generous in his division of household goods.
Comarques was put up for sale at the end of October, and almost
anything she asked for she was given, necessaries like the tea-
service, a couple of lustres, the window-curtains, and the bedroom
carpet, and some of the priceless manuscripts of his books.

Extracts from Marguérite's Journal—22nd November, 1921

At three o'clock today I signed the deed at my solicitor's. It
was presented to me sealed; I had to repeat after him what he
said. I swore what I was asked to swear. I had no reaction,
having prepared for this moment . . .

11 p.m. I am just back from the A.F.P.S. meeting which
took place at Miss Lion's. I have recited six sonnets by Ronsard

and three poems by Francis James. I was too tired to do myself justice ... Before interpreting Ronsard's sonnets I had to satisfy myself in imagining what Ronsard had experienced in his private life and what his attitude to life was. In fact I had to find out everything about him before I could breathe real life into the words he wrote. Such a method should always be used in a search for a penetrating and sensitive criticism and an understanding of the poet's mind.

No single instance better illustrates her extraordinary resilience than that, having signed her Deed of Separation in the afternoon, she should go on to give a recital of Ronsard in the evening.

Mutual goodwill and sympathy continued to exist between the two, perhaps more than when they had lived together. During the years she sent him presents of a muffler, newscuttings, and flowers, while he sent her tickets for theatre seats, New Year greetings, and copies of his books. She never really became convinced that one day he would not return to her. Two years after the separation she made a move towards seeing him, and received the following reply :

Mme. Arnold Bennett,   75, Cadogan Square,
12c, Upper Montague Street,   London, S.W.1.
London, W.1.   3.12.23.

Dear Marguérite,

 Thank you for your letter. I want you to believe that I have the kindliest feelings towards you, that I have no bitterness, and that I am willing to do everything I can to be of help to you. But you must allow me to have my point of view, just as you have yours. My point of view is that you ought to show courage and patience. You ought not to ask me to do something which would cause me very grave emotional disturbance and which in my opinion could at present lead to no good whatever. I certainly do not say that I will not see you later on but my feelings, as you probably know, are exceedingly quiet, profound, and *slow*. It takes me years to recover, *even partially*, from a

176

great crisis. You must be patient, you must have courage, and you must with good will resign yourself to the fact that in my opinion the time has not yet arrived for a meeting between us. If you can face this cheerfully there will be a better chance of us meeting, in a purely friendly manner, at a later date.

I have every sympathy with you. I understand your position. I want to help you. But I cannot undertake impossibilities. Follow my advice, and be patient, and as cheerful as you can. I have never yet given you bad advice. Go and see the Bions for a change. You want a change. Monotony and idleness are the worst things for you.

My very best wishes,

Yours, A.B.

The following year she received the following :

Mme. Arnold Bennett,   S.Y. *Marie-Marguérite*,
12c, Upper Montague Street,   Southampton.
London, W.1.   28.7.24.

Dear Marguérite,

Thank you for your letter, which I got on Saturday night at Ryde. I need not tell you that I should like to do everything possible for your happiness; but I am convinced that neither of us would be any happier if you returned to me. You doubtless think you would, but I feel sure that you would not. The old difficulties would very soon begin again, and I am not prepared to face them again. It is too soon. The past is still too fresh in my mind. You have your own friends. You have Robert (*Bion, her nephew*). You are a very clever woman; you have plenty of intellectual resources, and plenty of enterprise. When I last saw you I thought you looked extraordinarily young, vigorous, and beautiful. You have already created an existence for yourself, and if you set your mind to it you can go on creating more and more. I suggest that you should continue to work. This is unquestionably the best thing for you. It is not for me to advise you, but if I could advise you I should urge you to go

177

to France for a bit, and see your own people, who are all very nice.

I am glad you enjoyed the King's party,
                    With best wishes,
                              Yours sincerely,
                                        A.B.

One of the conditions of the Separation had been that she should not set foot in his home on penalty of losing her allowance. In March, 1931, when he was dying of typhoid, it was still in force, and in an hotel nearby she was writing in a shilling exercise-book :

Arnold is in the habit of sending me my quarterly allowance himself, to write to me a note each time, to write to me again for my birthday and Christmas. His messages I value immensely. Though possibly quite wrong, I imagine they are a token of his respect, affection for me. Loving him, I imagine that he still, in the secret of his heart, loves me . . . his messages were welcome, they secretly entertained in me the hope that he would come back to me—vain hope—yet hope that no disappointment, not even his present illness, can destroy. For years I have carried the hope to have a house in the country, where to retire when old and poorer, where I could, if circumstances would have it, receive my husband broken by illness or old age . . . A country home I now possess. I bought it last September. It is being fixed up for me. I am putting part of my savings into having this house [brought] up to date. With luck the repairs should be done by the end of June, and the house furnished and fit by August . . . I would then be able to entertain friends . . . and if, supposing Arnold were ill and incapable, he wanted to come and live there . . . he would find content, peace . . . perhaps happiness. He does not need my help now, he does not ask for me, but he might one day need me, and ask for me. Circumstances might bring him back to me in his old age.

He died the following day.

A *Writer's Diary* by Virginia Woolf

Arnold Bennett died last night; which leaves me sadder than I should have supposed. A loveable genuine man; impeded, somehow a little awkward in life; well-meaning; ponderous; kindly; coarse; knowing he was coarse; dimly floundering and feeling for something else; glutted with success; wounded in his feelings; avid; thick-lipped; prosaic intolerably; rather dignified, set upon writing, yet always taken in; deluded by splendour and success; but naive; an old bore; an egotist; much at the mercy of life for all his competence; a shopkeeper's view of literature; yet with all the rudiments, covered over with fat and prosperity and the desire for hideous Empire furniture; of gigantic absorbing power. These are the sort of things that I think by fits and starts this morning, as I sit journalising; I remember his determination to write 1,000 words daily; and how he trotted off to do it that night, and feel some sorrow that now he will never sit down and begin methodically covering his regulation number of pages in his workmanlike beautiful but dull hand.

Lolière, the country home referred to by Marguérite, stands near the small market-town of Negrepelisse, where she was born. Here she remained, apart from excursions abroad (notably in 1934 to England, vainly to contest Arnold's will) until her death in 1960 at the age of eighty-six.

Lolière became the background to her professed *vie de fantaisie,* about two acres of overgrown garden surrounding a Spanish-looking house cut off from a small farm by a high ornamental wall on which peacocks perched. The chief features were a long avenue of plane-trees, a magnolia as big as an old walnut-tree, and a pigeon-house of which the ground floor was a furnished flat to which in high summer Marguérite retired to write poems.

The focus of the estate was the small indeterminate yard outside the green front doors. Here ducklings waddled, cars came to a stop, the postman rested his bicycle; here too one came to listen to the nightingales or take one's breakfast or entertain visitors to afternoon tea. The window of Marguérite's study overlooked it so that she could keep an eye on the varied life dependent upon her: cats, ducks, hens, peacocks, pigeons, and guinea-fowl.

When one saw her of an evening with an old shawl round her shoulders, wearing a floppy straw hat with the odd flower or feather stuck into it, opening the fowl-pen gate and calling: 'Tuy, tuy, tuy!' the impression she gave was that she, who had acted as hostess to the political and stage celebrities of her time, who hoarded letters addressed to her from people as varied as Lord Roberts of Kandahar, the Aga Khan, and Edith Sitwell, was the farmer's mother come in from next door to lock up the poultry for the night.

In this house she gave poetry recitals. She was a cook, hostess often to a houseful of people, and after dinner she became a *grande dame* reclining on a settee in an out-dated black velvet dress and declaiming about things artistic, 'my poor Arnold', books, people and places seen, memories of the great days of old. Five minutes later, bringing another character into play, she would be off to shut up the ducks wearing the felt-lined boots in which Arnold had written 'The Pretty Lady'. (Why felt-lined? The explanation is that all writers suffer from cold feet.)

Her poems reflected her pastoral life in peace and war: *Un Coin de France, Diversité, Sur le Chemin de la Victoire,* and *Intimité.* In the first she wrote about Lolière, its trees, furniture, ghost, visitors, animals, pigeons, and river. Of *la Proprietáire* she wrote:

> Ame éternellement enfantine
> Amoureusement de la beauté
> Contemplative, un peu lascive,
> Fanatique de verité,
> Elle aime sa propriété
> En verite!

Which may be translated:

> Soul eternally childlike,
> A lover of beauty,
> Contemplative, a little sensual,
> Fanatical for truth—
> She loves her property,
> Indeed she does!

In spite of the liberties she took with her record of the past, she was indeed *fanatique de verité* in that when she questioned one, her black Spanish eyes gazed intently into one's own, and she would *burrow* after the truth until she got an answer. Then she would toss her head and laugh and say either : 'I knew it !' or 'That's impossible !' She welcomed all manner of guests, from an earthy agronomist who sat down to lunch in his braces, to the doctor's wife and the local pastor who were given tea with full honours in the garden. However, not until after she had died did the present editors discover that her relations lived all around her —Mme. Pons, the butcher's mother, a grocer, 'Mamie', the cousin who had helped to instal her at Lolière, a traveller in confectionery. Marguérite had just not cared to disclose their existence. On the other hand, in Montauban and Negrepelisse she would call out shopkeepers who were *not* her relations from behind their counters to shake hands with us.

It is not discoverable how or when she parted from M. Legros. Following the separation he disappears from the scene. Arnold once quoted him as asserting that an ambitious young man should always attach himself to an influential woman, and from the meagre evidence available it almost looks as though he had done just that, purely out of self-interest, and with nothing further to gain had taken his leave. On the other hand, we may be absolutely certain that Marguérite did not want to prejudice the allowance that Arnold was making her, or give him grounds for divorce, by letting herself be compromised. The situation might have been invented by Balzac.

Much of Lolière's furniture had come from Comarques, the 'hideous' Empire-style beds, chairs, and wash-stands, and many of the pictures, including the Cézanne-style portrait of Arnold by Edward Wolfe. Almost every one of Arnold's published works were contained in a tall glazed book-case, also from Comarques, with the three volumes of her *Resumé*.

She wanted in every way to be associated with Arnold, and continued to sign her passport : 'M. Marguérite Bennett (Mrs. Arnold Bennett)'. To us, her English relations, she poured out the difficulties of being married to genius (*'mon mari, le grand écrivian Anglais'*, was her pet phrase) and his grotesque mistake in separating from her. Sometimes she would be swept by uncontrollable storms of sobbing that might last for forty minutes, but whether they were due to remorse, or to Latin or poetic temperament, or to the hatred of Arnold that was also love, we were not to know.

She died in July, 1960, and lies buried among the Souliés, Hébrards and Villeneuves in the Protestant Cemetery at St. Antonin, *Tarn* et Garonne. Her memorial reads :

Ici Repose
Marie Marguérite Soulié
1874–1960
Veuve Arnold Bennett
Homme de Lettres Anglais

APPENDIX

One of Marguérite's letters in the original. A translation is given on pp. 143–5 and a photographic copy appears facing p. 113.

Grand Hotel,
Frascati,
10th April, 1921.

Mon cheri,

Il me semble que je suis plus que jamais une source de tourments continuels pour toi . . . si ce n'est pas Richard . . . c'est Legros . . . si ce n'est pas Legros . . . c'est des allusions que je fais sur des choses tangibles ou mystérieuses.

Si tu crois que c'est drôle pour une femme, de se sentir depuis pres de 14 ans, une enfant méchante, ou capricieuse ou mystérieuse; un être qui aurait du depuis le premier jour plier définitivement et devenir un être a ton image.—Car enfin c'est a quoi revient la source profonde des ennuis, des tourments, des insomnies dont tu es ma victime! Tu fais exactment et tu continue de faire comme John Read vis-a-vis de sa fille Emilie —et je pourrai te répondre ce que cette jeune personne (qui aussi en avait une couche!)"—It is not fair, one day you spoiled me and another day you are troublesome! . . .' (or whatever she said.)

Je passerai donc toujours ma vie à te faire souffrir et à te demander pardon! Il faut en effet que je suis une enfant et que j'en ai une couche!

Quand a Legros, je le connais encore mieux que toi . . . (illegible) aussi épaisse que soit ma couche, elle ne m'empêche pas de savoir exactement à quoi m'en tenir à son sujet. Je te remercie pourtant de toute la solicitude que tu me montres en voulant me protéger contre un homme jeune qui tu sais dangereux pour une personne de mon âge. Ce n'est pas parceque d'une façon générale les épouses anglaises voient tres peu leur maris, que cela a pu en quoi que ce soit m'aider a me résigner à voir si peu le mien. De plus, je ne suppose pas que tu te ranges dans la catégorie des hommes ordinaires.

J'ai reçu toutes tes lettres at les autres. Merci. J'ai fait part à Pierrot de ta lettre du 4 Avril. Il t'a écrit et, à son tour, me fait part de sa réponse. J'espère que toutes ces complications et ces malentendus disparaitront. Après tout, la vie est courte. Pourquoi ne pas nous la rendre la plus facile possible? Si nous n'y reussissons pas qui y reussira? N'oublie pas que dans l'ami que je protège il ya le soldat qui a suffert pendant 6 ans de la guerre; l'être un peu déséquilibré que l'amitié, l'encouragement, et la bonté et l'aide remettent petit a petit sur pied. Je me fais un devoir et un plaisir de le protéger, et je continuerai, tout au moins jusqu'a ce qu'il suit redevenu normal.

En m'occupant de lui, je ne t'enlève rien, je n'enlève a personne. En cela tu le sais aussi bien que moi.

Malgré un certain bouleversement que m'occasionnent tes lettres, je suis heureuse et satisfaite. Ma clairvoyance, ma sagesse, et ma philosophie, que tu prends pour une couche épaisse, les trois choses qui me rendent si mystérieuse à tes yeux, m'y aident. Je te parais mystérieuse parceque tu crois que je ne les possède pas.

Je t'en prie, sois heureux, ne te tourmente pas.

C'est avec plaisir que j'apprends que tu as fait connaissance d'une young musical comedy actress. Elles son légions les femmes que tu as charmées et qui tu charmeras. Je les reçois aussi chaleureusement que tu as reçois les amis hommes qui m'amirent ou à qui j'aime a rendre service. Tout devrait être pour le mieux; à mon avis tout est pour le mieux, mon pauvre chéri!

Je renonce à passer par Toulouse, voyage trop compliqué. Il a fait froid ces jours derniers. J'ai un peu de rhume que je soigne. Soigne-toi bien, mange bien, danse bien. J'ai bien reçu ton telegramme. Thanks. Je te bise.

Ta femme,
Marguérite.

ACKNOWLEDGMENTS

The Authors wish to thank Mr. Stanley O. Stewart, the Librarian, University of Keele, Staffordshire, and his staff, for their help and permission to quote from the following :

Correspondence between Arnold Bennett and his wife, Marguérite Arnold's Journal for 1906/7
Marguérite's typed Journal in English covering the period 22nd August 1920 to 31st December 1921, and her manuscript Journal covering the period 26th March to 22nd April 1931
Quotations from the above here appear in print for the first time Keele University Library's Occasional Publication No. 3, *My Association with Arnold Bennett,* by Frederick Marriott, 1967

The Authors are also under obligation to the following for permission to quote extracts relating to the marriage :

Mrs. Menetta Wainwright Morgan (Fredk. Marriott's *My Association with Arnold Bennett.*)
Macmillan & Co. Ltd (*The Merry Wives of Westminster,* by Mrs. Belloc-Lowndes, 1946)
A. M. Philpots Ltd. (*Arnold Bennett,* by Mrs. Arnold Bennett, 1925)
Ivor Nicholson & Watson Ltd. (*My Arnold Bennett,* by Marguérite, his wife, 1931)
Hogarth Press Ltd. (*A Writer's Diary,* by Virginia Woolf, edited by Leonard Woolf, 1953)
Allen and Unwin Ltd. (*My Seven Selves,* by Hamilton Fyfe, 1935)
To avoid repetition and irrelevance, the letters and other material have in many cases been abbreviated, but without in any way affecting the truth of their content.

All quotations from Arnold Bennett's letters and work appear by kind permission of his heirs. Invaluable help with detail has been given by Mr. K. D. Miller and Mr. John R. Ford, of the Stoke-on-Trent City Libraries, Miss Mary Kennerley, Mrs. Olive Glendinning, Anthony Rye, and Reginald G. Haggar R.I., whose comments and encouragement are hereby acknowledged with grateful thanks.

Alton, Hampshire   J.B.
England   G.B.